LOCKHEED F-104 STAR

Lockheed's legendary F-104 Starfighter enjoys a slightly dubious place in the annals of aviation history. Famous as one of the "Century Series" fighters, it was perhaps the least successful aircraft in this family, designed for a role that had changed quite drastically by the time that the F-104 emerged. Designer Kelly Johnson produced what was in effect a replacement for the F-86 Sabre, but with the Korean War at an end and the Cold War growing still colder, the USAF needed sophisticated all-weather fighters that could take-on Soviet bombers, not day fighters designed to take-on the MiG-15. This fact, compounded by early technical problems, soon encouraged the USAF to abandon its interest in the F-104 although Tactical Air Command's need for a nuclear strike aircraft gave the Starfighter a new lease of life – even if only for a few years. But it was overseas where the Starfighter eventually reigned supreme as a multi-role role warplane, becoming one of the most common and numerous types in Nato's inventory. Sadly, this popularity came at a price and the sheer numbers of aircraft in service, combined with the demanding environment in which the aircraft would operate, bestowed a grim accident record on the Starfighter which was almost impossible to shake off. In reality the F-104 was no more dangerous or unreliable than any of its contemporaries, but statistics can mislead and the Starfighter became famous as a demanding, potentially lethal machine. It was a lamentable outcome for an aeroplane that

pr...
b...
th...
Despite its unenviable (and undeserved) reputation, Lockheed's Starfighter was a hugely successful multi-role warplane that played a very significant part in the post-war era. Pretty impressive for an aeroplane that started-out as a simple lightweight MiG killer.

Tim McLelland
Series Editor
tim.mclelland@keypublishing.com

CONTENTS

For more than a century of aviation history and for further titles in this series, visit www.aeroplanemonthly.com

Photo: Tim McLelland

Cover Photo: USAF

Aeroplane Icons: F-104 STARFIGHTER
Editor Tim McLelland. **Design and Layout** Paul Silk.

Publisher and Managing Director Adrian Cox. **Executive Chairman** Richard Cox. **Commercial Director** Ann Saundry.

Distribution Seymour Distribution Ltd +44 (0)20 7429 4000. **Printing** Warners (Midlands) PLC, The Maltings, Manor Lane, Bourne, Lincs PE10 9PH.

ISBN 978-1-910415-20-7

Published by Key Publishing Ltd, PO Box 100, Stamford, Lincs PE19 1XQ.
Tel: +44 (0) 1780 755131. Fax: +44 (0) 1780 757261. Website: www.keypublishing.com

SABRE SUCCESSOR

The USAF enters the jet age and Lockheed embarks on a secret plan to build a new fighter

The Lockheed Starfighter was a direct result of America's combat experiences in Korea, where USAF fighter pilots found themselves pitted against the formidable MiG-15, a deceptively simple machine that possessed capabilities far beyond its relatively unsophisticated diminutive appearance. Despite the arrival of the legendary F-86 Sabre, the USAF never quite managed to fight on equal terms with the Soviet-built MiG-15 throughout the Korean conflict, and despite the unquestionable success of the F-86, the USAF inevitably began to look beyond the Sabre to the possibility of something better, long before the Korean War ended. The Lockheed Aircraft Company was at the forefront of this process. With its headquarters at Burbank near Los Angeles, Lockheed was already well established as one of America's leading aircraft design and manufacturing companies, with considerable expertise in the design of jet aircraft, thanks to the creation of the Lockheed Model 80 which had become the USAF's first jet fighter as the P-80 Shooting Star. Developed under the leadership of Clarence L. "Kelly" Johnson (a talented engineer already credited with much of the P-38 Lightning's design during World War Two), the P-80 was an unqualified success not only in terms of performance but also as an engineering project. It progressed from initial design to first flight in just 100 days, this breathtaking speed being not only testament to Lockheed's abilities, but also to the generosity of British manufacturer de Havilland who supplied a functional jet engine. Lockheed's experience with the Shooting Star led directly to the development of the Model L.153 (the XP-90) in response to a USAF requirement (issued in 1947) for a long-range penetration fighter and bomber escort. Two prototypes of the twin-engine XP-90 were constructed but the project was eventually abandoned when the USAF opted to pursue McDonnell's competing XF-88 Voodoo design, chiefly because Lockheed's XP-90 was seriously underpowered. Losing to McDonnell was a great disappointment to Lockheed's Advanced Development Projects department, but the XP-90 had undoubtedly provided a great deal of technical experience and it generated a wealth of useful knowledge that could be applied to new projects. When the USAF issued a new requirement for a new all-weather fighter interceptor during 1950, Lockheed immediately drew-up a design with which to meet the USAF's specifications, designated as Company Model L-205. Powered by two jet engines and armed with missiles and rockets, the project showed great promise but the USAF slowly began to lose interest in it, when the aircraft's projected weight inevitably began to increase and the aircraft's likely capabilities slowly began to look rather less exciting. Within a year the project had been cancelled, but early in 1952 another fighter development contract was offered to Lockheed, but this time the USAF demonstrated an astonishing lack of commercial wisdom, stipulating that the aircraft's design features must be patented by the USAF and that the aircraft would (if necessary) be manufactured by other companies. It was hardly surprising that Lockheed politely declined to pursue the

Lockheed's Burbank facility pictured during 1956, with various Neptunes and Constellations visible around the site. Today the airport still survives although most of the surrounding area has been developed quite significantly. It was at this site that Lockheed's design engineers first created what eventually became the F-104 Starfighter. *(Photo: Lockheed)*

Clarence Leonard "Kelly" Johnson contributed a great deal towards the design of the WWII-vintage P-38 Lightning and a long list of other well-known Lockheed aircraft. However, he is better known as the creator of the USAF's first jet aircraft, the P-80 Shooting Star. He is also credited with the initial design of the SR-71 Blackbird and U-2, and it was Johnson who was instrumental in setting-up a test site at Groom Lake in Nevada – now better known as the infamous Area 51. Johnson was the creator and driving force behind the Lockheed F-104 Starfighter. *(Photo: Lockheed)*

project, although there was one other key reason why Lockheed refused the development contract – the designers at Palmdale were already secretly working on their own fighter project.

Chief designer Kelly Johnson, together with Assistant Chief Engineer Hall Hibbard, had determined that they could create a completely new fighter design based on their own research, instead of merely responding to the USAF's requirements as they emerged. Johnson had started this initiative in 1951 when he visited South Korea to see for himself how well (or how inadequately)

Lockheed's P-80 Shooting Star was performing. He toured fifteen air bases and spoke to countless pilots, all of whom had accrued significant combat experience. The prevailing opinion was that the USAF's procurement chiefs were pursuing technology, placing their faith in the promise of missiles, duplicated controls, radar equipment and other systems that would undoubtedly increase the sophistication of every new fighter that emerged, but only at a price in terms of speed, altitude or agility. The pilots in Korea wanted something very different, explaining to Johnson that they

wanted simplicity. Encounters over Korea between Sabres and MiGs had served to emphasize the importance of maintaining a high standard of serviceability and reliability throughout all combat operations. A classic example of the Air Force's failure in this respect was provided by the Sabre's A-1CM gyro gunsight, which was so troublesome that Colonel. Francis Gabreski, (a WWII and Korean "ace") went on record as saying that he would rather sight his guns with the aid of a piece of chewing gum stuck on the aircraft's windscreen. This parlous state of affairs gradually gave rise to growing pressure for a

▲ The Lockheed P-80 was the USAF's first jet fighter, designed in 1943 under the leadership of Kelly Johnson. The Shooting Star was a simple design that performed well, although it was soon regarded as obsolescent. Experience in Korea soon demonstrated that the Shooting Star's design was no match for the swept-wing MiG-15, and the aircraft was soon replaced in theatre by the F-86 Sabre. Development of the jet fighter progressed with breathtaking speed and the USAF was soon looking towards a replacement for both the Shooting Star and Sabre, as was Lockheed's Kelly Johnson. It was Johnson's trip to Korea (where he closely examined Shooting Star and Sabre operations) that encouraged him to begin the design of a new fighter that would offer the USAF's pilots a much better capability. This eventually became the Starfighter. *(Photos: Aeroplane)*

Lockheed's Advanced Development Projects department is now famous as the "Skunk Works" although a great deal of the facility's work remains secret. The Starfighter was one of the first designs to be created by the Skunk Works team. The department moved from Burbank to Palmdale in 1990 and this skunk logo is now registered by Lockheed as the Skunk Works official company logo.

small, light and fast fighter that would out-perform the F-86 and the MiG-15. American combat pilots had become heartily sick of looking up at the undersides of MiGs, and the lightweight fighter concept was frequently regarded as panacea that would put its owners literally back on top. Some improvements eventually came into service, such as the A-4 gun sight, the "black box" components of which could be removed and replaced in a matter of minutes. However, the shortcomings in flying performance were more fundamental and it was these issues that gave rise to the air-superiority concept. Johnson's conclusion was that the USAF's fighter pilots did indeed require a fighter that was light and fast enough to out-perform any potential adversary. However he wasn't

entirely convinced by the concept of a "light fighter", even though the idea was already finding favour elsewhere, with Douglas developing what eventually became the diminutive A-4 Skyhawk, while across the Atlantic, Folland's Gnat was emerging, and in France the Dassault MD.550 was slowly being developed into the Mirage. But Johnson's common-sense approach prevailed, and he concluded that although the USAF might have a few top-notch men capable of performing well with sophisticated equipment, attention should be paid to the more typical "run-of-the-mill" pilot for whom a less-sophisticated light weight fighter might well have some advantages. His main objective would be to produce a relatively simple fighter that possessed good handling

qualities. The irony of this aspiration became evident many years later.

Johnson returned to his office at Lockheed and immediately embarked upon a completely new project to create a lightweight air superiority fighter for the USAF, even though at this stage the USAF had no such requirement. He was to be ably assisted by Project Engineer William Ralston (who had also worked on the P-80 and XF-90), and Experimental Department Chief of Engineering Arthur Vierick. The key aerodynamicist on the project was Rus Daniell, who had been responsible for the YF-94 Starfire project (a development of the P-80). Within a matter of weeks a relatively large group of engineers, aerodynamicists and technical experts had come together on

The swept-wing F-86 Sabre was a remarkably successful fighter, although it proved to be no better than the MiG-15 in the skies over Korea. USAF pilots became increasingly frustrated by the Mig-15's manoeuvrability, altitude capability and speed. Kelly Johnson discussed the Sabre's deficiencies with many USAF combat pilots and used his knowledge to design a completely new fighter that would offer the USAF a machine with drastically improved speed and altitude performance. The Starfighter was in effect a direct replacement for the Sabre. *(Photo: USAF)*

the new project, buried within what was now colloquially known as the "Skunk Works" within the company's Burbank headquarters. It is worth recording that the famous "Skunk Works" name can be traced back to 1943 and the company's XP-80 project. Because the war effort was in full swing there was no space available at the Lockheed facility for Johnson's design team, and they were obliged to operate in secret out of a rented circus tent next to a manufacturing plant that churned-out pungent fumes every day. Team engineer Irv Culver was a fan of newspaper comic strip "Li'l Abner" in which there was a running joke about a mysterious and malodorous place deep in the forest called the "Skonk Works" where a strong beverage was brewed from skunks, old shoes and other strange ingredients. One day, Culver answered a phone call by saying "Skonk Works, inside man Culver speaking." Fellow employees quickly adapted the name for their mysterious division of Lockheed and it is now an internationally recognized and patented name where many iconic aircraft were subsequently created, often in conditions of great secrecy. The Starfighter was one such example.

Developments in engine technology had

Assistant Chief Engineer Hall Hibbard was a key personality in the Starfighter's design process, working in close association with Kelly Johnson. He is seen with a model of the L-133, a design that was proposed to the USAF but abandoned because of its perceived complexity, leading to the production of the far simpler P-80 Shooting Star. *(Photo: Lockheed)*

now reached a stage at which it was feasible to produce a very capable fighter powered by just one afterburning engine, and the Lockheed team began design work on this basis. A great deal of research data and useful technical information was available from the USAF, US Navy and NACA (the forerunner of Nasa), including a great deal of material that could be gleaned from the Douglas X-3 Stiletto programme. This aircraft was being designed to investigate sustained supersonic flight behavior, utilizing an unusual low aspect ratio wing with a thickness-to-chord ratio of just 4.5 percent. The X-3's wing was certainly unusual when compared to the swept wing designs that had emerged over recent years, but it worked well during wind tunnel tests and pre-flight trials, and the short, stubby wings eventually became a fundamental part of the Starfighter's design, as did other features incorporated into the X-3 airframe, such as the smoothly-contoured engine intakes that blended into the fuselage sides, and the all-moving tailplane. Sadly, the X-3's full potential was never realized, thanks to the relatively low-powered engines with which it was equipped (the intended engines never materialized), but the X-3's design undoubtedly did have a significant influence

Lockheed's Model L.153 was developed by Kelly Johnson's design team in response to the USAF's requirement for a long-range penetration fighter and bomber escort (issued in 1947). The XP-90 (XF-90) was certainly an impressive design but when two examples were completed and flown, it was hampered by insufficient engine power. The USAF eventually abandoned the XF-90 in favour of McDonnell's Voodoo, but the entire requirement was subsequently cancelled. However, the XF-90 provided Lockheed's Skunk Works team with a great deal of technical data and experience, all of which was directly transferred to the F-104 programme. *(Photos: Lockheed)*

on the aircraft that Lockheed eventually produced. Lockheed also ran several thousand hours of aerodynamic tests in their own wind tunnels and in the Southern California Cooperative Tunnel, in which they had a one-sixth share. For the F-90 the company had made some use of ballistic models dropped from high altitude, but the terminal velocity attained was insufficient for the new fighter. Free-flight work was therefore entrusted to vehicles fitted with F-104 aerodynamic surfaces and launched from ramps in the desert under the thrust of 5in rocket motors, while more data also came from existing aircraft embodying components that were likely to be designed into the new fighter. Assistance was given by both NACA and Cornell University through the provision of variable stability aircraft capable of simulating the predicted behaviour of the Starfighter. Lockheed's designers were also well aware of NACA's "area rule" research, but it wasn't embodied in the new fighter's shape, as transonic interference drag was not expected to affect the Starfighter. Area rule is less applicable to what could be described as "wholly supersonic" aircraft, and with a remarkably small wing, the aircraft's fuselage would have

required little re-contouring to meet area rule principals in any case and in many respects it conformed to area rules principles almost by accident. The fuselage design was dominated by the overriding importance of obtaining optimum flow into (and out of) the turbojet engine, particularly when the engine was to expected to develop half its maximum-speed thrust as a ramjet. Supersonic air intake design was a complex subject that Lockheed had to explore thoroughly, in order to rid the aircraft of airflow boundary layer growth – something that is usually a function of fuselage length ahead of the intake. Lockheed also gathered valuable data from the X-7, a test vehicle that was designed by Irv Culver in order to investigate a variety of new ramjet designs. The X-7's ability to attain supersonic speeds

and altitudes in excess of 80,000ft made it an ideal platform with which to generate aerodynamic, flutter and structural performance data that would be directly applicable to the new fighter, and it was hardly a coincidence that the X-7 featured a wing and tail design that was remarkably similar to those that were being considered for the Starfighter. By 1960 the remarkable X-7 had claimed a record for an air-breathing vehicle, reaching a speed of Mach 4.31 and an altitude of 106,000ft.

The Skunk Works team drew-up more than 100 different design concepts for Johnson's new fighter, all of which where wholly or partially rejected. Initially, the aircraft started out (Model CL-227-0-6) as a relatively conventional design with wings that featured swept leading edges and

McDonnell's Voodoo played a significant part in the history of the Starfighter. It was the XF-88 Voodoo that eventually emerged victorious in the USAF's quest to acquire a new penetration fighter and bomber escort, beating Lockheed's XF-90. However, development of nuclear weaponry encouraged the USAF to look at very different bomber and fighter tactics, and this led to the abandonment of the requirement. The Voodoo re-emerged as the F-101 when the USAF revisited its bomber escort requirement some years later and it was the availability of the Voodoo (albeit in a greatly modified form) aircraft together with the F-102 and F-106, that ultimately convinced the USAF to lose interest in the Starfighter. The more sophisticated Voodoo, with radar and nuclear air-to-air missiles, promised better range and capability than the Starfighter. *(Photos: Aeroplane)*

un-swept trailing edges, combined with a swept tail and an engine intake placed centrally in the aircraft's nose, incorporating a fore-aft moveable shock cone. The design then progressed to feature a delta wing, although Johnson is on record as having never been particularly enthusiastic about delta wing designs and it was soon accepted that a delta would create unacceptable amounts of drag at the extremely high speeds that were anticipated. Within a few months the layout had been changed again to adopt the much smaller and thinner stub wings that were to be employed on the Douglas X-3, and from August 1952 the wing design was effectively fixed, while attention shifted to the rest of the aircraft. One important obstacle to overcome was the risk

of increasing weight, caused by the need to provide adequate range and performance. Inevitably this meant the incorporation of greater fuel capacity, and this led to a corresponding increase in structure that added more weight, thereby creating a need for even more fuel. This vicious circle caused the aircraft's predicted weight to rise to almost 50,000lb, but valiant efforts were made to bring the weight back down, and model CL-227-20-1 (October 1952) demonstrated this process, with weight drastically reducing to 25,000lb. Just four weeks later the design team had produced an even smaller aircraft with an empty weight of just 9,000lb, but by December 1952 the design had grown again and had become a 12,000lb machine (CL-246-1-1) that was

judged to be a good compromise between the many conflicting aerodynamic requirements that had been placed on the aircraft. Some further changes were made however, the most significant being the relocation of the tailplane to the top of the fin structure, in order to avoid inertia coupling risks. This change gave the fin so much authority that it would now create a significant rolling effect during turns, and so the stub wings were given anhedral in order to compensate for this effect. The finalized design was certainly unusual, with a long, slender fuselage combined with tiny un-swept wings, as if the aircraft was essentially a turbojet engine with minimal flying surfaces built around it. Of course this was in effect what Johnson and his team had

◀

The USAF's WS-303A "Weapon system requirement for a high performance tactical day fighter" led to a number of design proposals. Republic's bizarre XF-91 was developed into the AP-55 in order to meet this requirement but the design didn't proceed beyond the concept phase.
(Photo: Aeroplane)

▼

North American Aviation was well placed to secure the USAF's interest with their F-107, which was derived from their F-100 (the USAF's WS-303A requirement was regarded as a replacement for the F-100). However, the WS-303A requirement had in effect been written around Lockheed's proposal and it was no surprise that the F-107 was not pursued beyond the flight testing phase.
(Photo: Tim McLelland collection)

created. Despite having paid little attention to NACA's area rule principles, model CL-246-1-1 did now broadly conform to these requirements, with a gradual increase in frontal area progressing from the narrow nose, through the wider air intake profile, across the tiny wings (where the intake profile decreases), towards the tailplane structure. Lockheed Model L-246 was apporoved by Lockheed's management team during October 1952 and just a few weeks later Kelly Johnson (accompanied by project leader Bill Ralston and aerodynamicist Dick Heppe) visited Wright Patterson AFB to brief USAF officials. Johnson then went directly to the Pentagon to describe the project to General Don Putt, General Don Yates and Colonel Holloway, who acknowledged that

Northrop's N-102 Fang was a relatively unknown project that was created in response to the USAF's WS-303A requirement, but it did not proceed beyond the initial design phase and, as expected, Lockheed's fighter design emerged as the leading proposal. *(Photo: Tim McLelland collection)*

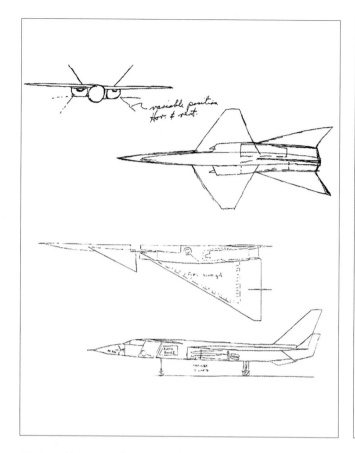

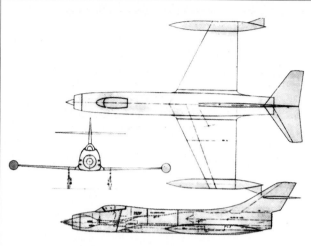

▲ This very early drawing shows how the design started-off with an intake configuration similar to that employed on the F-86 Sabre, although the intake cone was to be moveable both fore and aft, thereby varying the intake area.
(Photo: Lockheed)

◄ This rough sketch is believed to be one of the first drawings that Kelly Johnson produced, at the very beginning of the Starfighter project. Even at this stage, the distinctive wing design is clearly already in Johnson's mind, although an interesting canard wing design is also seen here on the same drawing.
(Photo: Lockheed)

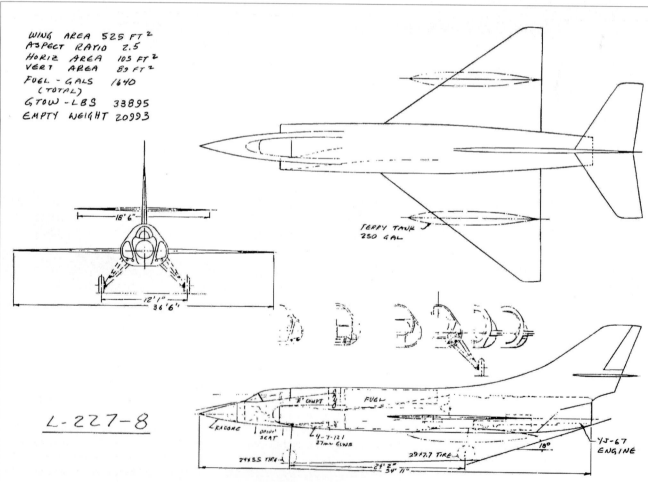

Design L-227-8 (April 1952) shows the delta wing design that was explored during the early days of the Starfighter project. By this stage the aircraft's size and weight had started to increase in order to meet the USAF's predicted performance requirements. The Starfighter's unusual main landing gear arrangement had already been established.
(Photo: Lockheed)

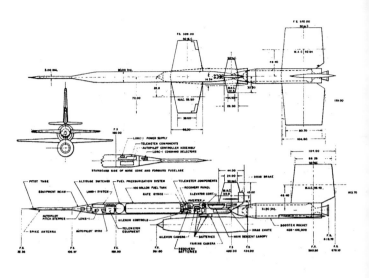

Lockheed's Irv Culver designed the X-7, a test bed vehicle capable of testing a number of early ram jet engines that were under development. With booster rockets power, the vehicle could reach altitudes of 100,000 feet or more, and speeds in excess of Mach 4.0, figures that were of obvious relevance to the new fighter design. The X-7 provided Lockheed with a wealth of aerodynamic and structural data and it was no coincidence that the Starfighter emerged with a wing and tail configuration that was largely similar to the X-7. *(Photos: Lockheed)*

the proposed design had great merit, however the USAF had no existing requirement for this or any other new fighter design. He suggested that Johnson should return at a later date, by which stage Holloway had written a brief Requirement document that specified a lightweight, high altitude and high-speed interceptor fighter, effectively written around the aircraft that Johnson and his team had designed. Unusually, instead of designing an aircraft to meet the USAF's requirements, the reverse situation had arisen in which the USAF had

drawn-up a requirement to match Lockheed's proposal. Armed with this important document, Johnson returned to Burbank to begin the process of turning the paper design into a functional machine.

Official USAF approval for the L-246 design (now designated as the Lockheed Model 83) was given in January 1953, and as a direct response to the USAF's WS-303A "Weapon system requirement for a high performance tactical day fighter" a contract for the production of two prototype aircraft followed on 1 March, with the USAF

designation XF-104. Ostensibly issued as a requirement for a F-100 Super Sabre replacement, other aircraft were submitted as potential candidates to meet the requirement. Republic drew-up the AP-55 (a development of the XF-91 Thunderceptor) while North American developed its F-100 into the F-107. Northrop produced the N-102 Fang, but Lockheed was identified as being the leading contender, not least because it had been Kelly Johnson's team that had effectively created the USAF's requirement in the first place. As described previously, the

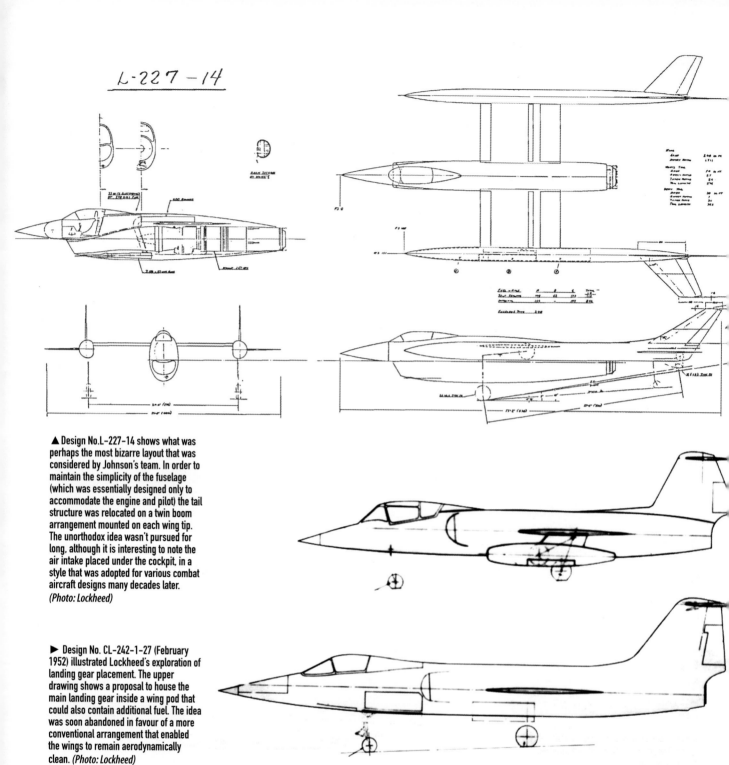

L-227-14

▲ Design No.L–227–14 shows what was perhaps the most bizarre layout that was considered by Johnson's team. In order to maintain the simplicity of the fuselage (which was essentially designed only to accommodate the engine and pilot) the tail structure was relocated on a twin boom arrangement mounted on each wing tip. The unorthodox idea wasn't pursued for long, although it is interesting to note the air intake placed under the cockpit, in a style that was adopted for various combat aircraft designs many decades later. *(Photo: Lockheed)*

▶ Design No. CL–242–1–27 (February 1952) illustrated Lockheed's exploration of landing gear placement. The upper drawing shows a proposal to house the main landing gear inside a wing pod that could also contain additional fuel. The idea was soon abandoned in favour of a more conventional arrangement that enabled the wings to remain aerodynamically clean. *(Photo: Lockheed)*

final Model 83 design was unashamedly based on the concept of minimalism, with dimensions largely dictated by the fixed size and weight of the jet engine. The engine almost completely filled the available space within the airframe, and Lockheed had to work hard to find room for sufficient fuel capacity. Their solution gave the impression that they had figuratively poured fuel all around the intakes, ducting and powerplant, and then sealed it up in fireproof bays. The Model 83 fuselage carried more fuel than did the twin-engine Lightning long-range fighter of World War Two vintage, and Lockheed confidently described the new aircraft as having range "comparable to that of present operational jet fighters" although this was

perhaps an optimistic claim when in reality the aircraft was short of fuel capacity from the outset. In some respects it was almost inconvenient for Lockheed's designers that provision had to be made for a human pilot in the Model 83, when their X-7 was unencumbered by such accessories. Even though the pilot was to wear a T-1 partial pressure suit, his cockpit had to be pressurized and air-conditioned, and means had to be provided for his escape in emergency. The result was a great deal of additional structure and weight that was necessary to simply accommodate the pilot. Lockheed concluded that the optimum escape arrangement was to employ a type of automatic downward-firing ejection seat that

had already used by Strategic Air Command that not only eliminated the possibility of the pilot hitting the aircraft's fin or tailplane upon exit, but permitted a simpler (lighter) canopy and a less-complicated cockpit structure. Lockheed also carefully studied an escape capsule concept (leading to many ill-informed reports that some sort of astronaut training system was being devised), but after extensive testing the increased weight and complexity of successfully separating the aircraft's nose section from the rest of the airframe was judged to be a prohibitively difficult and expensive exercise, while the more conventional ejection seat also provided an escape hatch that could be removed so that with the seat withdrawn

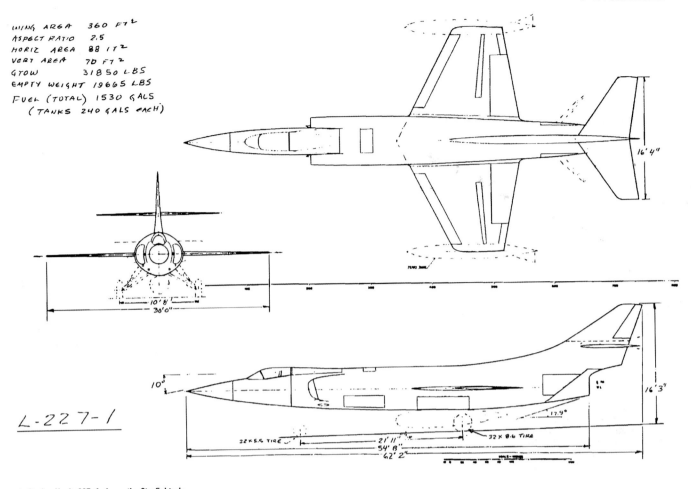

WING AREA   360 FT²
ASPECT RATIO   2.5
HORIZ AREA   88 FT²
VERT AREA   70 FT²
GTOW   31850 LBS
EMPTY WEIGHT 19665 LBS
FUEL (TOTAL) 1530 GALS
    (TANKS 240 GALS EACH)

L-227-1

▲ Design No. L-227-1 shows the Starfighter's familiar wing layout but with a very different tail structure with a swept tail fin and a tailplane positioned ad mid-height. However the Starfighter's intake configuration is shown, with intakes positioned either side of the fuselage, leading through internal ducting to the engine compressor. (Photo: Lockheed)

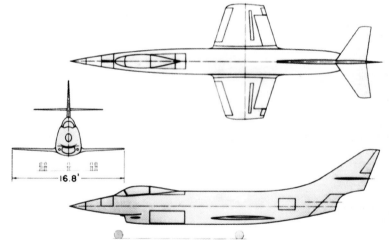

▶ Design CL-227-16-2 was one of the first drawings to adopt the wing layout that was eventually chosen for the Starfighter. At this stage however, the air intake was still placed centrally under the forward fuselage. At this stage the overall proportions of the aircraft had been reduced drastically in order to save weight and restore the aircraft's predicted performance. (Photo: Lockheed)

there would be stand-up working space in the cockpit for ground crew technicians (maintenance requirements received particular attention and were regarded as an important part of the aircraft's design). Virtually all the radio and electronics systems were packaged into readily removable units, the idea being carried to its logical conclusion by the evolution of several standard "mission configurations" suited to the electronic requirements of a particular mission. Another aid to servicing was the grouping of all the centralized hydraulic components on the inside of the large access door under the engine compartment. A conventional undercarriage system was adopted, with small tyres inflated to approximately 300lb/sq

in. Each main leg featured a forged cantilever hinged along an oblique axis to one of the main engine-support frames. The leg was also hinged along a horizontal axis to enable it to deflect outwards under landing loads, under the restraint of a vertical shock-strut. Each unit retracted forwards hydraulically into bays closed by two doors on each side, each rear door being linked to its appropriate leg. Anti-skid, multi-disc brakes were incorporated into each main-wheel, with the static discs being restrained by external torque links. The steerable nose wheel retracted rearwards into an unpressurized box sealed by twin doors. Landing lights and taxying lamps were mounted on the nose leg and inside the main-wheel doors.

The most striking feature of the Model 83 was it's remarkably small wing. Because of predicted high bending moments in the wing (which, as a result of the extreme thinness, generate unprecedented root stresses per foot of chord) it seemed likely that Lockheed would have to make the wing as a single slab from tip to tip. This in turn dictated a low wing-position in order to clear the crowded fuselage interior. However, as the design progressed it was found possible to make the fuselage frames strong enough to take out all the wing loads, each semi-wing being cantilevered (missile-fashion) from the fuselage. It was therefore practical to adopt a mid-wing arrangement with a 12 per cent reduction in drag over that of the low-wing

The Douglas X-3 Stiletto played an important part in the Starfighter's story. Designed to explore sustained supersonic flight, it was anticipated that the aircraft would achieve speeds in excess of 2,000mph but it suffered from poor engine performance and proved incapable of even attaining Mach 1.0 in level flight. However, the aircraft featured the same wing design that Johnson's team chose for the F-104 and the X-3 provided Lockheed with a huge amount of flight data and many aspects of the X-3's design were used to refine the layout and structure of the Starfighter. *(Photo: Tim McLelland collection)*

layout. Each half-wing projected from the fuselage intersection line to a distance of just under eight feet. As this was approximately the same as the height of the vertical tail above the fuselage, the rudder had considerable influence on rolling behaviour and this necessitated the incorporation of ten degrees of anhedral in each wing. The short span was inevitable because the thickness/chord ratio had to be low. Such wings were the optimum form for the high-supersonic regime in which the F-104 would ideally perform, and where considerations of induced drag cease to have their subsonic importance. However at lower speeds, older rules applied and as the aircraft produced greater span loading than any other combat aircraft at that time, induced drag became serious towards the lower end of the speed range and particularly acute at high altitudes. This put the aircraft in a category of aircraft where enormous performance existed at high

altitude and high supersonic speed, but where the medium-altitude and medium-speed conditions left poor reserves for climb and acceleration. The Model 83 was expected to get through to the upper limits of speed and altitude in a matter of a few minutes, and so the considerations of medium-altitude and medium-speed were less of an issue, and the question of how the aircraft would perform at low altitude was not examined in any great detail, although attention was certainly paid to the aircraft's low-speed handling characteristics. In order to improve wing behaviour at high angles of attack, the leading edge could be drooped by some 20 degrees. Johnson's design team also introduced what was then an entirely new concept, in the shape of Boundary Layer Control (BLC); this system drew air from the engine and fed it though thin vents across the wing trailing edge flaps, thereby restoring airflow separation that would otherwise occur at low speed. This

system reduced the landing speed by more than 17 knots and would enable the aircraft to achieve 25 percent shorter landing distances than would have been possible through the use of more conventional high lift devices (without BLC, the aircraft's landing speed was later estimated at an eye-watering 240 knots). It would enable pilots to fly the aircraft comfortably with a full load at speeds under 200 knots which, although my no means a pedestrian speed, was commendably low for an aircraft that was designed for supersonic flight (it should also be mentioned that the leading-edge drooping mechanism was accommodated in a maximum interior depth of less than 2in, which was quite an achievement). The supersonic aerodynamic profile of the wing was complex, involving flats and smooth curves joined by a 0.016in nose radius and a knife-edge at the rear. Such a profile could generate high lift at low angles of attack and, with the leading edge drooped, could

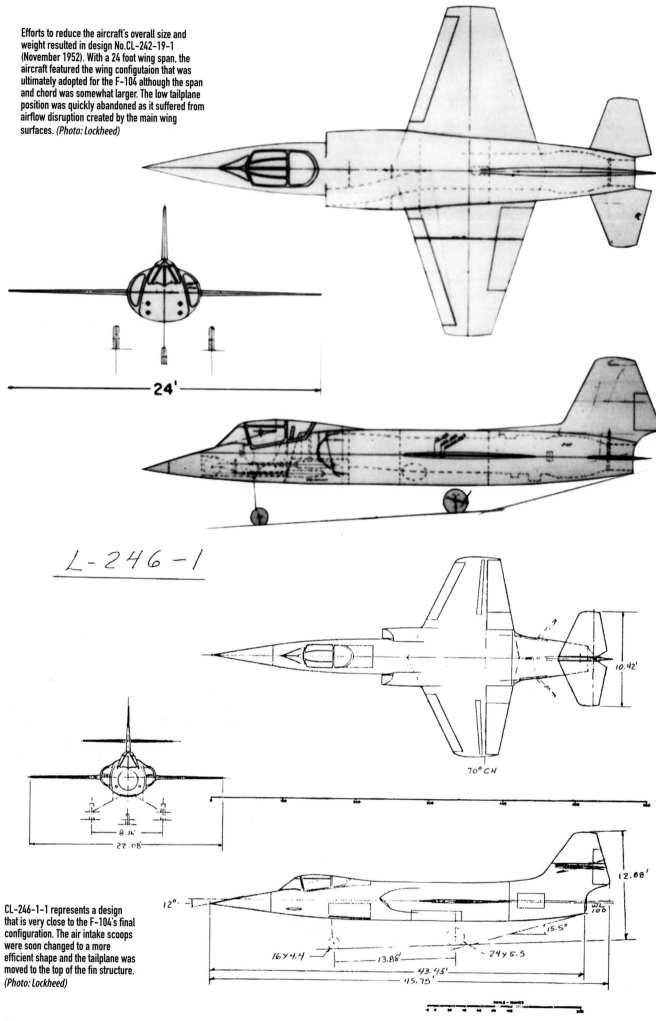

Efforts to reduce the aircraft's overall size and weight resulted in design No.CL-242-19-1 (November 1952). With a 24 foot wing span, the aircraft featured the wing configutaion that was ultimately adopted for the F-104 although the span and chord was somewhat larger. The low tailplane position was quickly abandoned as it suffered from airflow disruption created by the main wing surfaces. *(Photo: Lockheed)*

24'

L-246-1

10.42'

70° CH

22.08'

8.16'

12.08'

12°

16 X 4.4

13.88'

15.5'

24 X 5.5

43.45'

45.75'

CL-246-1-1 represents a design that is very close to the F-104's final configuration. The air intake scoops were soon changed to a more efficient shape and the tailplane was moved to the top of the fin structure. *(Photo: Lockheed)*

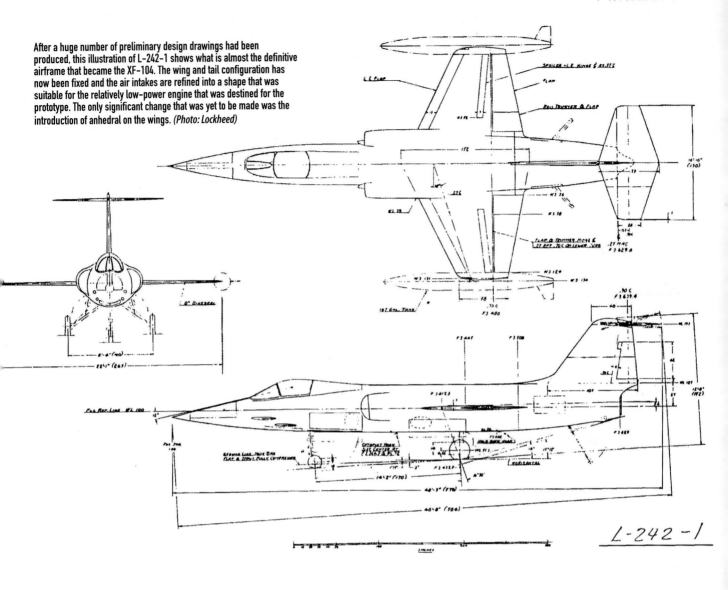

After a huge number of preliminary design drawings had been produced, this illustration of L-242-1 shows what is almost the definitive airframe that became the XF-104. The wing and tail configuration has now been fixed and the air intakes are refined into a shape that was suitable for the relatively low-power engine that was destined for the prototype. The only significant change that was yet to be made was the introduction of anhedral on the wings. (Photo: Lockheed)

L-242-1

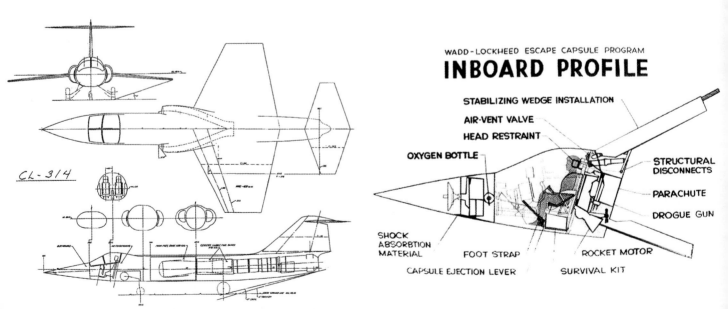

During the preliminary design process, Johnson's team looked at potential designs for a dual-control variant of the aircraft. Some consideration was given to this interesting side-by-side seating configuration although when work on the twin-seat aircraft began, it was abandoned in favour of a much simpler tandem seating arrangement that required much less modification to the existing single-seat design. (Photo: Lockheed)

Lockheed devoted a great deal of time and effort into the possibility of producing an escape capsule for the aircraft, although tests soon revealed that the complexity and weight of the system would make it impractical for a combat aircraft such as the F-104 and a more conventional ejection seat was eventually adopted. (Photo: Lockheed)

reach reasonable lift coefficients, although in this respect it obviously could not match subsonic wings. Wing loading on the Starfighter was quite considerable, but even at low speeds the fuselage generated substantial lift.

The primary armament for the new fighter would be a single General Electric T-171-E3 Vulcan six-barrel 20mm rotary cannon (subsequently designated as the M61A1), positioned in the forward port fuselage. Electrically powered to fire at a rate of 3,000 or 6,000 rounds per minute, it would carry 725 rounds of ammunition and would be linked to a Type K-19 Fire Control System, with AN/APG-34 radar and a computing gun sight. If the cannon was not required, the entire armament fit could be replaced by an additional 120 US Gallon fuel tank, although external fuel tanks were designed for carriage on weapon stations under each wing. Jettisonable fuel tanks, each carrying 200 US gallons, could also be fitted over the wing tips like gloves, and although these tanks increased supersonic interference drag, they exerted a beneficial end-plate effect equivalent to an increase in span. Without these tanks, each wing tip could carry a Philco Sidewinder, then known as the GAR-8 and subsequently re-designated as the AIM-9B. Span-wise flow on a straight wing is negligible, so no wing fences were required. Despite the projected high performance of the aircraft, the Starfighter's control system was remarkably conventional. Moments of inertia in supersonic aircraft are usually much larger in yaw and pitch than in the rolling plane, and cross coupling between these moments had recently killed George Welch (engineering test pilot of North American Aviation) whilst flying an early F-100 Super Sabre. Results of the ensuing investigations were distributed throughout the US aviation industry and this tragic accident may well have saved Lockheed from similar difficulties. Rolling control was achieved through the use of large-chord, small-span ailerons that were operated hydraulically without tabs. Control in the pitching plane was provided by a slab tailplane hinged at its mid-chord point near the tip of the fin. In this position it formed a useful end plate, and Lockheed calculated that the Model 83's fin was approximately twice as effective as equivalent areas on other fighters. Structural problems in the tail's design were considerable, but any other arrangement would have placed the tailplane in a fluctuating downwash and in the path of shock waves, therefore the high-mounted position was judged to be the optimum solution. With a thin straight wing the aircraft's centre of gravity needed to be forward of the 20 percent chord position. As the centre of gravity travels aft in the transonic regime a considerable nose-down pitching moment is introduced, which must

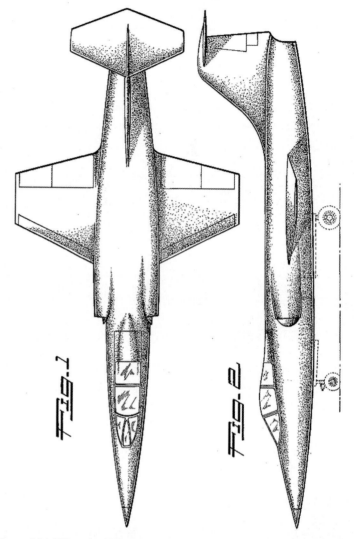

United States Patent Office

Des. 179,348
Patented Dec. 4, 1956

179,348
AIRPLANE

Clarence L. Johnson, Encino, Calif., assignor to Lockheed Aircraft Corporation, Burbank, Calif.

Application April 22, 1954, Serial No. 30,122

Term of patent 14 years

(Cl. D71—1)

This document dated 4 December 1956 effectively marks the very beginning of the XF–104 aircraft, when Kelly Johnson submitted this general arrangement drawing to the US Patent Office. *(Photo: Lockheed)*

be counteracted by a downward force on the tailplane, therefore it is not surprising that Lockheed considered a canard wing layout during the initial design process, although the idea was swiftly abandoned in favour of a more conventional (and simpler) configuration. Inboard of the ailerons were large-chord split flaps that provided a considerable amount of lift, while air brakes were hinged on each side of the rear fuselage, designed to bring the aircraft's speed down with some considerable force, when fully deployed. In order to keep landing distances within a reasonable scale, a ribbon-type braking parachute was located in a box under the engine afterburner assembly. Throughout the structural design process, Lockheed strived to create an

airframe capable of cheap and rapid production. The wing was machined almost completely with much of the structure being of steel, not only to accommodate kinetic heating, but because the use of light alloy would have placed too much of the material too close to the aircraft's neutral axis point to achieve any weight advantages. Control surfaces and access doors were conventional sheet assemblies stabilized by a filling of Lockfoam and parts of the skin were integrally stiffened. Lockheed claimed that the airframe cost roughly half as much as the structures of its contemporaries, although this was partly due to the fact that the Model 83 was only half as heavy. By contemporary standards, the Model 83 was a strikingly small and light machine. ❖

Lockheed F-104 production begins at Lockheed's Palmdale plant in California.
(Photo: Lockheed)

INTO SERVICE

The F-104A is introduced into USAF service and Lockheed's first export customers receive the Starfighter.

The two Starfighter prototypes were manufactured with astonishing speed and a wooden mock-up of the XF-104 was completed in April 1953. By January 1954 the first XF-104 (Lockheed 083-1001 s/n 53-7786) was ready for transportation from Burbank, out to Edwards AFB in the Californian desert. Because the predicted development of a suitable jet engine was proving to be a slower process than Lockheed had anticipated, the first aircraft was equipped with the most powerful engine that was readily available, in this case a Curtiss-Wright XJ65-W-6 turbojet (a licence-built Armstrong Siddeley Sapphire) developing 7,200lb thrust. The engine was far from ideal, but the XF-104 airframe weighed only 11,500lb, and test pilot Tony LeVier reported that the aircraft performed well during its maiden flight, completed on 4 March (although a short "hop" along the lake bed had taken place on 28 February), even though he was unable to explore the aircraft's capabilities in any detail, thanks to the malfunctioning of the landing gear. Because the gear refused to fully retract on the first flight, LeVier opted to perform a low-speed handling flight of around 20 minutes, and further attempts to fly were similarly hampered until low hydraulic pressure was identified as the cause of the undercarriage retraction problem. After a period of bad weather, test flying resumed on 26 March when the landing gear retracted properly and a full flight testing programme began, although it was some seven months before 7786 was joined by the arrival of the second prototype (53-7787, making its first flight on 5 October) equipped with a more powerful Wright J65-W-7 engine that incorporated an afterburner system. This engine was also retrofitted to the first prototype and on 25 March 1955 test pilot J. Ray Goudey attained a speed of Mach 1.79 at 60,000ft in the second aircraft. As an armament trials aircraft, this airframe was also equipped with the Vulcan cannon system, and with a more powerful engine the aircraft was able to exceed Mach 1.0 with ease, whereas the first prototype (before the engine refit) was only capable of exceeding the speed of sound in a shallow dive. The initial gun firing tests with the Vulcan cannon on the second aircraft were successful, but on 17 December there was a major incident during a firing test and when a loud explosion was heard, during which the J65 engine suffered severe compressor stalls. Tony LeVier immediately shut down the engine and glided back to Edwards AFB to make a successful dead stick landing on the Rogers Dry Lake. Investigations revealed that one of the 20mm cannon rounds had exploded inside the breech, blowing the bolt out the rear of the gun and through the surrounding structure into the forward fuselage fuel cell. Jet fuel had run into the

gun bay, and leaked out of the compartment door seals and into the left engine air intake. The engine had immediately flooded with fuel, causing the compressor stalls. Thankfully, this was the only serious incident during the Vulcan cannon's flight trials but 53-7787 was ultimately destroyed by its own Vulcan cannon on 14 April 1955, after being abandoned high over California. Test pilot Herman Salmon was performing gun trials at 50,000ft when the gun malfunctioned during a test firing, causing severe vibrations to build up inside the cockpit. The vibrations dislodged the ejection hatch in the cockpit floor and cabin pressure was lost, with Salmon's pressure suit inflating and covering his face so that he could no longer see.

Recalling LeVier's harrowing experience with the exploding cannon shell a few weeks previously, Salmon believed that the same thing was happening to him and that ejection was his best option. He later learned that instead of ejecting he could have simply descended to lower altitude, thereby allowing his pressure suit to deflate. The loss of the armament test bed forced Lockheed engineers were forced to find an alternative, and subsequent trials were continued with a modified F-94C Starfire. Sadly, the first prototype was also lost a couple of years later, although by this stage it was no longer assigned to test flying and had become a chase aircraft for production-standard Starfighters. On 11 July 1957 it developed tail

(Above & Left) — Lockheed's test pilot Tony LeVier posing for publicity images atop 53-7786, the first XF-104, seen at Edwards AFB during 1954. *(Photos: Lockheed)*

fin flutter during a test chase flight and the entire tail section was ripped from the fuselage, forcing test pilot Bull Park to eject. Oddly, the risk of tail fin flutter had already been established and the prototype had been restricted to a top speed of Mach 0.95, while Tony LeVier had already recommended that the aircraft should have been withdrawn from use. Although the incident ended without casualties, it meant that both historic prototypes of the Starfighter had now been destroyed.

On 17 February 1956, the USAF ordered 17 pre-production YF-104 aircraft (s/n 55-2955 to 2971), all of which would be equipped with the General Electric J79-GE-3a turbojet. This was the engine that Johnson and his team had anticipated throughout the aircraft's design process, promising to deliver a much more satisfactory 9,600lb thrust, or 14,800lb with afterburner. The dimensions of the J79 required Lockheed to modify the XF-104 airframe quite significantly, and the fuselage was stretched from 49.17ft to 54.77ft, thereby increasing the startling appearance of the aircraft's stubby wings still further. The tail fin was enlarged slightly and strengthened, increasing overall height from 12.7ft to 13.49ft. A less obvious change was the switch from a rearwards-retracting nose wheel to a forward-retraction version, and the addition of a dorsal fuselage spine, allowing control runs to be moved from inside the fuselage, thereby creating more space for fuel. As planned, the engine air intakes were redesigned to accommodate the greater demands of the more powerful J79, and the greater speeds that it would bestow upon the aircraft. The simple intake "cheek" plates fitted to the prototypes were changed to inlet "bullet" cones with internal bleed slots (designed to divert air for afterburner cooling), which were better suited to the greater air mass flow created by the J79. Surprisingly, despite having been flying for two years, the general public and media were still unaware of the Starfighter's existence until the USAF released official photographs of the second YF-104A being rolled out (55-2956) on 16 February 1954. A

The prototype XF-104 is seen at Edwards AFB on the Rogers Dry Lake during high speed runs that were conducted late in February 1954, just days before the maiden flight was completed on 4 March. *(Photo: Lockheed)*

great deal of speculation had been growing within aerospace media circles about the possibility of Lockheed producing a revolutionary new fighter, but the USAF made strenuous efforts to keep the project secret, in line with standard security arrangements that applied during the early Cold War era. USAF officials were astonished and angered when a Japanese magazine published a remarkably accurate artist's drawing of the rumoured aircraft, and even when the first official photographs were taken, specially-manufactured metal shrouds were fitted over the aircraft's air intakes so that their true proportions could not be seen; the USAF suspected that any talented aerodynamicist would be able to estimate

the aircraft's speed performance by examining the new air intake design. With maximum take-off weight increased slightly to 15,700lb, the first YF-104A (55-2955) was completed at Burbank early in February 1956 and after being transported to Edwards AFB, it made its first flight on 17 February in the hands of test pilot Herman "Fish" Salmon, just one day after the second aircraft had been unveiled to the public. On 27 April the YF-104A achieved a speed in excess of Mach 2.0 during a test flight from Edwards AFB and after only a few more months of evaluation, the USAF issued a contract for 146 F-104A aircraft, on 14 October.

Compared to the in-service YF-104A test aircraft, production F-104A Starfighters

featured a strengthened airframe that was stressed for manoeuvring up to 7.33g. An aft-mounted ventral fin was fitted to the centerline to improve directional stability at high speeds and high altitudes and improved flap blowing BLC systems were installed. Because of the revolutionary boundary layer control system, the landing speed of the F-104A was only five percent higher than that of other contemporary fighters. The BLC operated in connection with the wing flaps so that when the flaps passed the fifteen-degree mark during extension, the bleed air valves began to open and reached a fully open position when the flaps were all the way down at 45 degrees. The highly compressed air needed

Colour photographs of the XF-104 prototype are rare. These images were captured at Edwards AFB some time after the aircraft's first flight. By this stage the national insignia had been repainted on the aircraft's intake fairings. The side view clearly illustrates the shorter fuselage of the XF-104 as compared to the production-standard F-104A. *(Photo: Lockheed)*

to operate the system was taken from the 17th compressor stage of the J79 engine and ducted into the wing and out over the upper flap surfaces via a set of 55 slots fixed along the trailing edge flap hinge line. Full-span leading-edge flaps operated in conjunction with the trailing edge flaps for take off, landing, and low-speed manoeuvring. The aileron system was interconnected with the flap so that when the flaps were fully raised, aileron travel was limited to 65 percent. The entire horizontal stabilizer was pivoted aft of the fin mid-chord line and moved as a single unit so that there was no need for a separate elevator. An automatic pitch control system provided advance warning of an impending stall; as the stall approached, the system energized a stick shaker to warn the pilot. If the pilot ignored the warning and persisted in maintaining the same attitude and speed, the system was designed to automatically apply a forward stick force. An interim-standard AN/ASG-14T-1 radar fire control system was also fitted to the F-104A, and this was subsequently replaced by a more

capable AN/ASG-14T-2 fire control system in later aircraft. The first 35 F-104As delivered to the USAF were assigned to further test flying during which changes and improvements were progressively introduced in new batches of aircraft batches coming off the production line. It was an important process that served to develop the Starfighter into a more reliable and capable machine but it inevitably had an effect on the USAF's procurement schedule. The F-104A had originally been scheduled to replace Tactical Air Command's F-100 Super Sabres beginning in 1956, but by the time that the F-104A was declared ready for delivery in any significant quantity, the Air Force's requirements had changed quite significantly. The Starfighter's primary role as a high-speed interceptor fighter endowed the aircraft with a relatively low endurance, and its inability to carry a significant offensive weapons load made it largely unsuitable for TAC, where it was scheduled to replace the F-100. Although there is little evidence of TAC's honest view of the

Starfighter programme, it seems likely that the aircraft was in effect imposed upon the Command because the concept of a replacement for the F-100 seemed like the most plausible justification for the USAF's purchase of the F-104A, when (as explained previously) the USAF never had any clear requirement for the aircraft. Air Defense Command already had their own fighter and interceptor aircraft under development, and although TAC would certainly require a replacement for the F-100, a more versatile fighter would be needed that could carry much bigger and more varied external loads. Consequently TAC had expressed its lack of interest in the F-104A long before it actually entered service. However, delays in the delivery of the Convair F-106 Delta Dart were becoming a major concern for Air Defense Command, and the availability of the F-104 (especially now that TAC had expressed reservations) provided an obvious "stop-gap" solution to ADC's problems. The F-104 lacked endurance that and it had no all-weather capability, but its high rate of climb was a

A magnificent photograph of the first XF-104, pictured high over the Mjave desert during a test flight from Edwards AFB. The prototype's simple air intakes are clearly visible — these were soon modified to incorporate the Starfighter's distinctive inlet cones that were necessary for the greater speeds provided by production-standard engines. *(Photo: Lockheed)*

distinct asset that could provide ADC with a very capable fighter until the new F-106 became available. It was hardly the most glamorous or auspicious entry into service for any new warplane, but it was certainly better than premature abandonment.

The first USAF unit to receive the F-104A was the 83rd Fighter Interceptor Squadron based at Hamilton AFB in California, where the first aircraft arrived during February 1958. Next to re-equip with the Starfighter was 56th FIS based at Wright-Patterson AFB in Ohio, followed by the 337th FIS based at Westover AFB in Massachusetts. Finally, the 538th FIS based at Larson AFB in Washington also received the Starfighter. Early service experience with the aircraft proved to be a challenging time, and the Starfighter soon proved to be a troublesome machine. The

F-104A aircraft was equipped with either the J79-GE-3 engine or the later J79-GE-3A. By modern standards both versions of the engine were crude early models, and it was probably inevitable that they would be unreliable in service. They were directly responsible for several crashes and in-flight emergencies during the first years of the Starfighter's existence, with flameouts, oil depletions, rough-running and ignition failures often occurring, much to the frustration of ADC's pilots and the maintenance crews who were obliged to rectify the many problems. The engine problems eventually resulted in the grounding of all F-104As during April of 1958 so that further accidents could be avoided while a thorough investigation of the Starfighter's problems could be conducted.

Most of the engine failures were eventually traced to problems with the J79's variable-geometry afterburner nozzle system – a complicated assembly that produced the all-important reheat performance (and also produced some bizarre harmonic sounds that were to fascinate observers and enthusiasts for decades to come). But when the afterburner system was selected, the nozzle was inclined to stick in the open position after being turned off, and this restricted available engine power to an equivalent output of little more than idle thrust. This was insufficient to maintain level flight, and the Starfighter's hapless pilot was inevitably obliged to abandon the aircraft because of this relatively simple snag. The early F-104As lacked a modulated afterburning system, meaning that the

engine could only deliver either full dry power or full afterburner, which effectively meant a level speed choice of either Mach 1 or Mach 2.2. Thankfully, a more reliable version of the J79 was soon developed in the shape of the J79-GE-3B rated at 9,600lb thrust or 14,800lb with afterburning, and this was retrofitted to the existing F-104As from April 1958. The F-104As were returned to flight status in July 1958 although the safety record of the F-104A continued to concern USAF officials, being significantly higher than figures applicable to other contemporary fighters. Serious accidents and crashes continued, some being attributed to control issues (and pilot error) although most were still a result of engine malfunctions.

During June 1958, English Electric's Chief Test Pilot Roland Beaumont was afforded an opportunity to fly an F-104A. He was unashamedly critical of the Starfighter, claiming that the aircraft had inadequate directional damping, evidenced by a persistent low-amplitude short-period oscillation throughout most of the flight regime. He also reported that the small and thin, highly-loaded wing had a severe adverse effect on the aircraft's turning maneuverability. There were excessive break-out forces of the power-controlled ailerons and at high angles of attack, the high-set stabilator (combined tailplane and elevator) would tend to stall in the wing's downwash, creating a sudden departure into a potentially fatal flat spin. Recovery from such the flat spin was usually possible only if there was sufficient height so that increased engine power could be applied to accelerate the aircraft back into controlled flight, but the Starfighter's rapid rate of descent in such conditions meant that ejection was often the only sensible option. Beaumont found that subsonic handling properties were poor and particularly dangerous in take off and landing configuration, and he believed that the aircraft was unsuitable for operation in poor weather conditions. He predicted that the F-104 was likely to suffer a high accident rate during its operational life, although other observers regarded his findings as being overly critical, perhaps because the F-104 was potentially a commercial competitor for English Electric's Lighting, an aircraft that was being designed to undertake the same high speed and high-level fighter role. Aside from issues concerning the airframe and engine, the

53-7786 is seen here carrying wingtip fuel tanks during early trials conducted from Edwards AFB. Because of tank oscillation problems, various tip tank tail fin designs were tested before a standard arrangement was established for production fuel tanks, although in this photograph the tanks are devoid of any such modifications. Clearly visible is the upper fuselage, clearly scuffed by ground maintenance crews. The Starfighter's distinctive fuselage spine was not introduced until production of the F-104A began. (Photo: Lockheed)

Despite flying for the first time in March 1954, it wasn't until April 1956 that the XF-104 was first unveiled to the media. At this stage the aircraft's performance was still a closely guarded secret and Lockheed believed that examination of the aircraft's intake design would enable observers to estimate the aircraft's capabilities, and so the intakes were covered with conformal shrouds while the aircraft was on show. *(Photo: Lockheed)*

▶ This impressive view of the XF-104 prototype shows the aircraft later in its test programme, now carrying modified wingtip fuel tanks with horizontal stabilizing fins. The wing surfaces have also been sprayed gloss white — this became a standard arrangement for all unpainted Starfighters although there is little evidence to explain why. The white paint probably reduced the temperature of the wing structure at high speeds. *(Photo: Lockheed)*

M61 Vulcan cannon fitted to the F-104A demonstrated excessive vibration during firing and occasionally suffered from premature detonation of its 20mm shells. The cannon had also performed badly under high-g conditions during testing and in November 1957 the USAF decided that the cannon should no longer be installed in any more production F-104As, and that it should be removed from existing F-104As until the many problems could be fixed. Consequently, for quite some time ADC's Starfighters were operated without any cannon armament being installed, relying completely on the wingtip-mounted Sidewinder missiles as their only armament. It wasn't until 1964 that the cannon was improved, enabling the more reliable M61A1 be made available, so that the F-104A fleet could finally receive full armament.

As described previously, the F-104A was fitted with a Lockheed-designed ejection seat that fired downwards from a hatch under the cockpit. Lockheed engineers had feared that upward-firing ejections would be unsafe at the phenomenal speeds that the F-104 would attain, and it was believed (on the basis of a great deal of testing) that the seat would be unable to clear the tall vertical tail at such speeds. The downward-firing

ejection system seemed like a logical solution and although a similar design had already been used by Strategic Air Command, it was the first fully-automatic downward-firing ejection system ever employed in a production fighter. When the pilot initiated the ejection sequence by pulling the seat's ejection ring, an automatic sequence of events was initiated; Firstly, the

cockpit depressurized and the flight control stick retracted. The parachute shoulder harness then tightened and the pilot's feet were pulled together and clamped into place. The escape hatch then blew clear from the bottom of the aircraft and the seat fired, ejecting the pilot out the bottom of the airplane within seconds. However, the seat was useless for escape if the aircraft was

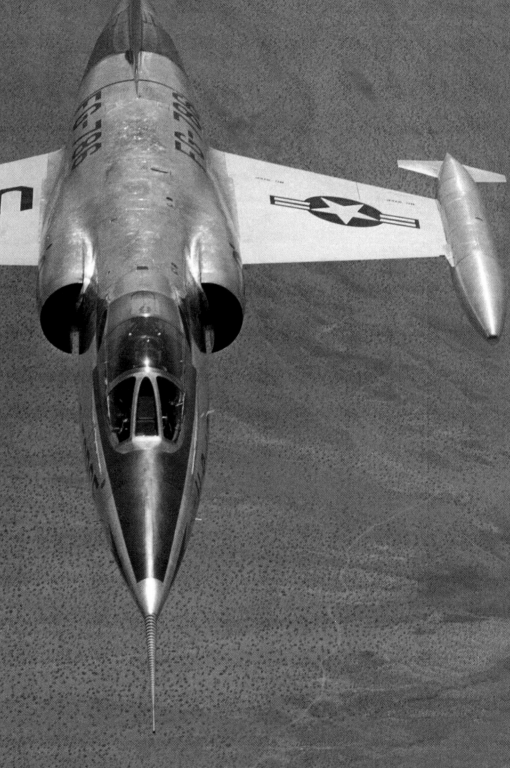

A rare image of the two XF-104 prototypes together over Edwards AFB, shortly before the second aircraft (53-7787) was destroyed on 18 April 1955 when test pilot Herman Salmon abandoned the aircraft following the loss of the aircraft's escape hatch. *(Photo: Lockheed)*

The second XF-104 was the first to be equipped with the Wright J65-W-7 engine, which enabled the aircraft to attain a speed of Mach 1.79 on 25 March 1955. This was the highest speed achieved by either prototype. *(Photo: Lockheed)*

operating at a low altitude, particularly during take-off and landing when the aircraft was in its most vulnerable flight regime. The only means of using the seat at low level was to roll the aircraft inverted before ejection – something that would be impossible at low speed. No less than 21 F-104 pilots were killed because of the system's shortcomings, and within a matter of weeks the USAF's new F-104 pilots were expressing severe misgivings about the ejection seat. It prompted the USAF and Lockheed to swiftly look for a more conventional system and Lockheed C-2 upward-firing ejection seats were progressively fitted to the Starfighter fleet as soon as they became available, leaving the Starfighter's unique cockpit hatch as a curious relic of the original design, useful only for easy maintenance access.

In 1959 the USAF announced that the F-104A would be withdrawn from ADC service, ostensibly on the grounds of incompatibility with the SAGE (Semi Automatic Ground Environment) air defence network that had been set-up for ADC's operations, and because the Starfighter was both short-ranged and incapable of all-weather operations. However there is no doubt that the Starfighter's troubled entry into service had done little to convince ADC that the aircraft was worth keeping, and with more sophisticated F-106 and F-101 aircraft in the pipeline, the F-104A's fate was probably sealed during two weeks in October-November 1959 when no less than five aircraft were lost in flying accidents. Air Defense Command's F-104As were transferred to three Air National Guard squadrons during 1960, the 151st FIS of the Tennessee ANG, the 157th FIS of the South Carolina ANG, and the 197th FIS of the Arizona ANG. These three ANG F-104A units were soon selected for active duty during the Cold War's Berlin crisis in 1961 and they were deployed across the Atlantic to bases in France and Germany. They returned to the USA in 1962 and most reverted to state control although some were retained by the USAF and were transferred to two ADC units (the 319th and 331st FIS at Homestead AFB in Florida) as part of the 32nd Air Division. Rather oddly, these two squadrons exchanged their sophisticated all-weather F-102s and F-106s for the troublesome (and less capable) F-104A, and although no logical reason for this seemingly retrograde step was given, the aircraft remained in service for several years. From late 1967, 26 aircraft from the 319th FIS were retrofitted with a more powerful J79-GE-19, rated at 17,900lb with afterburner, and the last USAF ADC squadron to operate the F-104A (the 319th FIS) disbanded in December 1969, marking the end of the type's service with active duty squadrons. The F-104A had been a disappointment both for Lockheed and the USAF. Designed without the USAF's

This publicity photograph of the second XF-104 illustrates the unusual downward-firing ejection seat that Lockheed adopted for the Starfighter. The seat was designed to fire through an escape hatch built into the cockpit floor, ensuring that the pilot would not strike the aircraft's tail fin. However the system was clearly unsuitable for operation at low altitude. *(Photo: Lockheed)*

knowledge or input, Lockheed had created a remarkably capable fighter that could attain great speed and great altitude. It was the machine that Kelly Johnson had envisaged - an aerial supremacy fighter that would have easily prevailed in the skies over Korea, but by the time that it was designed and manufactured the Korean War had ended and the USAF was already looking towards more versatile designs. The Starfighter was a useful temporary acquisition for ADC but its temperamental engine, demanding handling qualities and potentially useless escape system, often made it more of a problem than an asset. Ironically, it was not within the

USAF that the F-104A performed its most useful function; During October 1958 twelve F-104As from the 83rd FIS at Hamilton AFB were dismantled and airlifted by C-124 transport to Taiwan, where they served temporarily with the Republic of China Air Force during the Quemoy (or Taiwan Strait) crisis. The crisis was peacefully resolved and the aircraft were eventually returned to the USA, although little information on this deployment was ever released. The USAF's F-104A fleet was effectively redundant by 1962 even though some aircraft soldiered-on for another seven years with ADC (as described above) and others went on to

◄ ►

Lockheed's Palmdale facility pictured during 1957. As can be seen, production of the F–104A was underway with numerous Starfighters visible outside the flight test hangar, which is visible in the foreground (at an oblique angle). In the background the two huge assembly hangars can also be seen. The hot and dry conditions at Palmdale enabled engineers to work on aircraft outdoors, and various aircraft can be seen with their tail sections removed, enabling engineers to gain access to the J79 engine. (Photos: Lockheed)

▼

The first YF–104A was 55–2955, completed in January 1956 and flown for the first time on 17 February in the hands of Harman Salmon. The aircraft was destroyed on 25 April 1957 when test pilot Jack Simpson failed to lower the aircraft's landing gear in time for a hurried landing at Palmdale. The aircraft skidded off the runway although Simpson walked away unscathed. (Photo: Tim McLelland collection)

perform second-line roles. In 1960, following the decision to withdraw the Starfighter from ADC service, some 24 F-104A aircraft (which had already been declared surplus to USAF requirements) were modified to QF-104A standard as radio-controlled target drones. Painted in a dazzling fluorescent orange finish (with white wings), the aircraft were operated by the 3205th Drone Squadron at Eglin AFB in Florida as airborne targets for missile firing exercises. Although the QF-104A could be flown conventionally with a pilot in the cockpit, they were usually flown remotely, either with a controller flying in a director aircraft, or by controllers based on the ground at Eglin AFB. Either way, the task of handling this very demanding aircraft by remote control was no mean feat, but the drone fleet was operated successfully for many years until most of the aircraft had been destroyed.

In all, some 153 F-104As were manufactured in seven production blocks (F-104A-1-LO to F-104A-30-LO) and the last F-104A was delivered in December 1958. The number of aircraft manufactured was far less than had been anticipated by Lockheed and only 170 F-104As and YF-104As were ultimately acquired from of the 722 that had originally been proposed. Shortages of funds (due to the needs of other programmes) accounted for some of this reduction, although the decision by TAC not to adopt the F-104A was the main reason why the production total was cut so short. Some F-104As were released for export, and the air forces of Taiwan, Pakistan, and Jordan were eventually equipped with former USAF

F-104As while the rest (excluding those converted to drone configuration) went to Davis-Monthan AFB in Arizona for storage and eventual disposal. One example (56-770) was loaned to the Royal Canadian Air Force as the design model aircraft for what eventually became the Canadian export version of the Starfighter (Canadian serial number was 12700), while a further three aircraft (56-756, 56-760 and 560-762) were modified as NF-104A aerospace pilot trainers. Two F-104As (56-734 and 56-749) were transferred to NACA in October 1957 and these were used as high-speed chase aircraft. 56-749 crashed in December of 1962 and a third F-104A (56-790) was transferred to NASA in December 1966 (the F-104A remained in use with Nasa into the 1980s). Despite it's disappointing tenure of service with the USAF, the YF-104A was undoubtedly an impressive machine. During December 1958 a Lockheed F-104A flown alternately by Lt. William T. Smith and Einar K. Enevoldson (over a two-day period at NAS Point Mugu in California) set several time-to-climb records, including 9,842ft in 41.35 seconds, 49,212ft in 131.1 seconds, and 82,020ft in 266.03 seconds. This breathtaking capability might well have been used to advantage had plans to create an unarmed photographic reconnaissance version of the aircraft been pursued further, after work on this variant began in November 1954. Designated as the RF-104A (Model 383-93-04), a contract for eighteen aircraft (56-939 to 56-956) was issued, but as the USAF's confidence and interest in the F-104 began to wane, the project lost momentum and the contract

was cancelled in January 1957.

Other than the short assignment of aircraft to the Republic of China, the first overseas customer for the F-104 Starfighter was Pakistan. Following the withdrawal of the F-104A from service with the USAF's ADC, a batch of F-104A aircraft (plus two dual-control trainers) was supplied to the Pakistan Air Force (PAF) under the US Mutual Defence Assistance Programme. They entered service during 1961 and continued to fly until 1972 when dwindling spares support forced their early retirement. Twelve F-104As were delivered, these being 56-803 to 807, 868, 874, 875, 877, 879, 773 and 798, plus trainers 57-1309 and 1312. In response to Pakistan's requirements, all of the F-104As were refitted with the M-61 Gatling 20mm gun that had previously been removed from most F-104A airframes because of reliability issues. Pakistan had considered the exclusive use of the aircraft's Sidewinder missile armament but the decision to re-fit the cannon system proved to be a wise move, as the aircraft were soon being used in actual combat. The improved J79-GE-11A engine (designed to be stall-free and to deliver a maximum thrust of 15,800lb) was also installed in the aircraft. This made the Pakistan F-104s somewhat unique in that despite carrying cannon armament, they were still the lightest of the F-104 series whilst being equipped with a more advanced J79 engine, thereby enjoying an excellent thrust-to-weight ratio. The only PAF unit to be equipped with the F-104 was No.9 Air Superiority Squadron, a unit that had

On 7 May 1958 Captain Walt Irwin claimed new speed and altitude records in YF-104A 55-2969, nicknamed "Speedy". He reached 3,000m from take-off in 41.8 seconds, 25,000m in 4min 26.03secs, and a speed of 1,404mph over a course at Edwards AFB, and was awarded an official Fédération Aéronautique Internationale (FAI) World Speed Record. This was the first time that one aircraft held both a world speed and world altitude record simultaneously. 55-2969 was returned to its parent unit (the 83rd TFS) but subsequently loaned to General Electric from August 1958 for engine development work. At this stage it was renamed "Queenie". *(Photos: USAF and General Electric)*

F-104A 56-0739 was delivered to the USAF's Flight Test Center at Edwards AFB on 29 June 29 1957. Assigned to various test units, the aircraft never entered squadron service, and eventually it was converted to QF-104A drone configuration. Based at Eglin AFB, it was shot down on 8 October 8 1963 by a GAR-2B missile. *(Photo: USAF)*

previously operated ancient Hawker Fury fighters, and although the jump from the biplane era was drastic, the unit's experience with the Starfighter was very positive. The serviceability rate of the F-104A during the first five years of service was over 80 percent and the aircraft performed well throughout its operational life. Employed in the medium and high level air-to-air role by the PAF, the F-104A Starfighters remained in service for twelve years and flew some 11,690 hours. During the 1965 Pakistan-India War, the F-104s flew a total of 246 hours and during the 1971 War, the F-104s flew a total of 103 hours. During the first of these two conflicts,

the Pakistan Air Force was forced to use its small force of Starfighters as high altitude interceptors in both day and night fighting roles, using the aircraft's AN/ASG-14T1 fire-control system in conjunction with Sidewinder air-to-air missiles. From 1 September onwards, the F-104s were employed more extensively in air defence and air superiority operations, and from the 246 missions flown by F-104s during hostilities, 42 were at flown at night against the Indian Air Force's Canberras. The F-104A's relatively unsophisticated fire-control radar was more than adequate for the Soviet high altitude bomber threat for which it was

designed, but it could not illuminate small targets against ground clutter, making it less-than ideal for anything other than high-altitude interception. Therefore the standard high speed intercept tactic employed by PAF's F-104 pilots was to approach their targets from below, with a typical height differential of between 2,000 and 3,000 feet, against a target that they would acquire at a range of 10-15 kilometers. This tactic was well known to the Canberra jet bomber pilots of the IAF who flew the attack missions into Pakistan, and they adopted a standard hi-lo-hi profile to minimize the threat of interception.

From the seventeen YF-104As that were manufactured, only two are known to have survived intact. The seventh YF-104A (55-2961) was transferred to the National Advisory Committee for Aeronautics (NACA) in August 1956. It was initially numbered 018, but subsequently changed to civilian registration N818NA. In 1958, NACA was reorganized as NASA, and the YF-104A remained with NASA until November 1975. After a period of storage the aircraft is now in the National Air and Space Museum in Washington DC. *(Photo: Nasa)*

During most of their inbound and outbound flight over Pakistani territory the IAF Canberras would stay below 1,000ft during their approach and exit phases. This posed a difficult night intercept problem that required the F-104A to be flown in an unconventional low-altitude intercept profile that severely challenged the capabilities of its airborne radar. To pick up the low flying bombers on their radar scopes, the F-104 pilots had to get down to less than 500ft to point their radars upwards and clear of ground clutter, towards the enemy bombers. The PAF's problems were aggravated by the Canberra's tail warning audio alarm that

would sound as soon as Starfighter got anywhere near a line-astern astern position, enabling the bomber pilot to take timely evasive action and shake-off his pursuer. But despite the Starfighter's limitations, the Indian Air Force's pilots regarded the F-104 as a very serious threat. On 3 September 1965, even before the War began, an Indian Gnat pilot surrendered to an F-104 pilot, who forced the Gnat pilot to land at an abandoned airfield at Pasrur in Pakistan. On 6 September two Starfighters were sent on dawn patrol from Sargodha. They were vectored towards a flight of four IAF Mysteres engaged in bomb and rocket

attacks against a stationary passenger train at Gakkhar railway station. One of the F-104 pilots was forced to return to base with a radio failure but the second pilot put his F-104 into a dive in full afterburner power, plunging supersonically through the Mystere formation (which promptly scattered.) The Indian pilots tried to escape at very low level but they couldn't escape the Starfighter. One Mystere was hit by a Sidewinder missile and became a victim of one of the world's first air victories by a Mach 2 combat aircraft. The other F-104 pilot,who had missed his chance the previous day, enjoyed greater success on 7 September when he was scrambled in an

Testing of the AIM-9B Sidewinder missile for the was conducted at NAF China Lake, using three YF-104s transferred from the USAF, together with additional F-104A aircraft temporarily re-assigned from the USAF. F-104A 56-0748 was one such aircraft. Trials revealed that carriage of only one missile could cause a dangerous rolling tendency at low speeds and for operational use it was recommended that if missiles were to be carried, a Sidewinder should be attached to both wings for formation take-off. *(Photo: USAF)*

F-104A 56-0737 was delivered to the USAF's ARDC (Air Research and Development Center) at Edwards AFB, in May 24 1957. A year later it was assigned to NAF China Lake and the Navy Missile Center (NMC) for supersonic Sidewinder missile tests. It was eventually converted to QF-104A standard and shot down by an AIM-9 missile on 3 July 1972. *(Photos: USAF)*

This Lockheed publicity photograph shows two of Lockheed's classic aircraft, both of which were keeping Lockheed's production facilities busy during the 1950s. The P-2 Neptune is accompanied by an F-104A from the ARDC for a formation rendezvous near Edwards AFB. *(Photo: Lockheed)*

F-104A at 05:15 hours and directed by radar towards an incoming raid at Sargodha. He made visual contact with the IAF Mysteres and headed towards them. By the time he caught up with them, the Indian aircraft were roughly eight miles away from Sargodha, flying at 150 feet on a south-easterly heading towards India. As the Mystere pilots jettisoned their drop tanks, he positioned himself behind one Mystere and released a GAR-8 missile, which went straight into the ground. The Mystere pilot immediately began to employ evasive tactics and a full "dogfight" ensued, with the Starfighter pilot using the F-104A's superior climb and acceleration to lift the combat from ground level to more than 7,000ft in order to gain room for manoeuvre, but allowing the F-104 to get into a turning fight

was a mistake. The Mystere pilot showed commendable courage by staying in the fight, and despite being mortally wounded he eventually scored several cannon strikes against the Starfighter, causing it to be abandoned. This was the first and only Starfighter to be lost through enemy action in the 1965 war, and the incident served to illustrate that in less-than ideal circumstances, the Starfighter was still vulnerable to older and less-capable fighters. The Indian pilot (Squadron Leader A.B. Devayya) was posthumously awarded the Maha Vir Chakra in 1988, some 23 years after the war, when Indian authorities learned of the event through an account of the encounter published in John Fricker's book "Battle for Pakistan." Another Starfighter had already been lost on the previous night

when its pilot inadvertently flew into the ground whilst attempting a landing approach in a dust storm over Peshawar, although the pilot managed to survive, having been thrown clear of the aircraft during the impact. On 21 September, an Indian Air Force Canberra was intercepted at 33,000ft and shot down with a Sidewinder. The bomber's pilot ejected and was made a POW while the navigator was unable to bail out and was killed in action. This was the first "kill" achieved by an F-104A at night after a number of near misses. F-104s were also used during 1965 for low level, daylight reconnaissance missions over the IAF's air bases. The speed of the Starfighter gave the Indians no time to react to each incursion, effectively making the Starfighters invulnerable to interception. The F-104s were

F–104As 56–0769 and 56–0781 from Air Defense Command's 83rd Fighter Interceptor Squadron, based at Hamilton AFB, California, pictured over San Francisco harbor. F–104A No.56–0769 was accepted by the USAF on 6 November 1957. Following a period of USAF service, as part of project "Ali Shan No.1" it was transferred to Taiwan during November 1960 and became "4208" of the 8th TFS/3 Wing. *(Photo: Lockheed)*

The Republic of China Air Force (RoCAF) received the first of 24 former USAF F-104As in 1960. Eventually, Taiwan became one of the largest operators of the Starfighter, acquiring aircraft from American and overseas operators, and it is believed that more than 240 examples were delivered in total. *(Illustration by Ted Williams)*

Ten former USAF F-104As (and a pair of dual control trainers) were delivered to Pakistan in 1961. Joining the Pakistan Air Force's No.9 squadron, they were used in combat on numerous occasions, the first encounters with Indian forces occurring in 1965. *(Illustration by Ted Williams)*

A batch of 36 Starfighters was allocated to Jordan in April 1966 but the 1967 Six Day War resulted in a delay in deliveries and it wasn't until 1969 that the aircraft joined the Royal Jordanian Air Force. Further F-104As were delivered in 1969-70 and the type remained in service until 1982. *(Illustration by Ted Williams)*

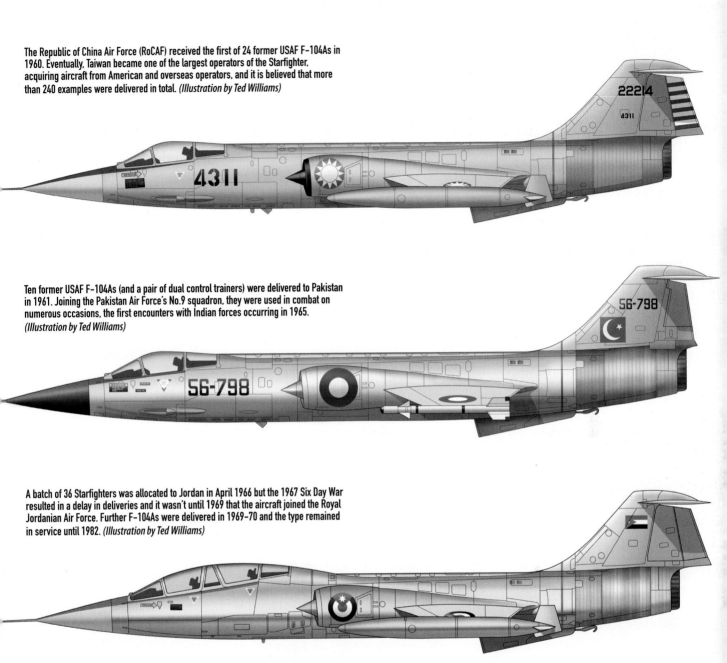

also employed as escorts for the much slower Lockheed RT-33 reconnaissance fighters that were used for photographic missions deep into India's territory, the presence of Starfighters virtually guaranteeing that no air opposition would be encountered. Six F-104 pilots received gallantry awards during the 1965 War and a few years later the Starfighter went into battle yet again after a second conflict began in 1971. This time the F-104A was also used for deep penetration strikes against enemy airfields and radar. It was no surprise that the United States Government imposed an embargo on further arms sales to both India and Pakistan as soon as the 1965 war had started. Little consideration was given to the practicalities of this action, and it ignored the fact that India was a long-time ally of the Soviet Union, using very little American military equipment, meaning

that the sanctions degraded the ability of only the Pakistani Armed Forces. The PAF fleet of F-104s was severely affected by the arms embargoes and it soon became increasingly difficult to maintain a serviceable fleet of aircraft. By 1972 the PAF concluded that it was no longer possible to keep the Starfighters in service in any significant quantity and so the F-104A fleet was withdrawn. Without restrictions of spares and other support, it is possible that Pakistan's F-104A aircraft might have remained active for at least another decade - something that would have been quite remarkable for a machine that had suffered such a troubled beginning.

F-104As were also supplied to the Republic of China Air Force and two of these aircraft were transferred to Pakistan as replacements for the machines that had been lost during the first conflict with India.

Further Starfighters were also supplied to the Royal Jordanian Air Force, with 18 machines being delivered during 1969. At least ten aircraft were temporarily transferred to Pakistan during hostilities in 1971 although few details have emerged about the role played by these aircraft, and it is not known if they participated in combat missions against Indian aircraft. It is also open to question whether they were flown by Pakistan's or Jordan's pilots. However, it is believed that two F-104As were shot down on the last day of the conflict on 17 December, and although loss claims vary, it seems likely that five PAF aircraft and four Jordanian aircraft were ultimately lost during the Starfighter's time in service. Unlike Pakistan, Jordan (free of any arms embargo) maintained its Starfighter fleet until 1975 when Mirages were finally introduced as replacements. ❖

HIGHER AND FURTHER

Tactical Air Command takes the Starfighter to Vietnam and Lockheed secures the European Sale of the Century

Despite the F-104's inauspicious beginnings, Lockheed continued to put their resources into development of the aircraft. Tactical Air Command's decision to abandon the Starfighter was a major setback the programme and this may well have been a fatal bow had it not been for a sudden change in fortunes. The F-104A clearly lacked the range and endurance that TAC required, and having been designed for the air-to-air role, it wasn't capable of carrying the heavy air-to-ground weapons loads that TAC required. But it was also true that procurement of new aircraft types for TAC was a difficult process, not least because TAC was often unsure as to which aircraft might be the most suitable for its continually shifting requirements. With the F-100 Super Sabre coming into TAC service, the F-104A had been identified as an eventual replacement, but the more versatile F-105 Thunderchief was also under development, and it was the prospect of this new machine that eventually discouraged TAC from pursuing the F-104A. Despite this, TAC eventually concluded that the original contract for 56 Starfighters (placed on 2 March 1956) should be retained, even though a later contract for a batch of reconnaissance-configured aircraft should still remain cancelled. TAC's volte-face was the result of growing delays in the F-105 programme and the acceptance that even with many deficiencies, the Starfighters might fill a perceived capability gap between the slower F-100 and the Mach two Thunderchief. Just as

The less-than successful introduction of the F-104A into USAF service resulted in the Starfighter's swift departure from front-line service. However the F-104A fleet was re-allocated to Air National Guard units and the aircraft remained in use for some time, pending the arrival of the more sophisticated F-102 and F-106. *(Photo: Tim Mclelland collection)*

importantly, the Starfighter would be perfectly suited to the carriage of a tactical nuclear bomb, and it was this possibility that finally persuaded TAC to rekindle its interest in the F-104. The order for 56 F-104C-5-LO aircraft was later increased to 77 when a second contract for 21 more was approved on 26 December 26 1956 although this figure was still significantly lower than the initial plan for a further 363 examples. The first F-104C (unofficially designated as the YF-104C) took off on its maiden flight on 24 July 1958. The F-104C was powered by the General Electric J79-GE-7 engine rated at

10,000lb thrust (or 15,800lb with afterburner), a figure that represented an increase of almost 1,000lb when compared to the earlier J79-GE-3A/3B used by the F-104A (the increase in power was achieved by increasing the diameter of some turbine blades by just over 2in.) Range was improved drastically through the provision of a fixed (removable) in-flight refuelling probe that could be attached to the port side of the fuselage. Fundamental to TAC's decision to acquire a small fleet of Starfighters was (as explained previously) the F-104C's ability to carry tactical nuclear weapons, one of which could

Lockheed test pilot Lou Schalk delivers the first F-104C to Tactical Air Command on 16 October 1958. Wearing the multi-coloured markings of the 479th TFW, the aircraft also wears the name "Really George" in recognition of the Wing's commander George Laven, and the aircraft's first home, George AFB in California. Unusually, the aircraft was also treated to specially painted white-walled tyres. *(Photo: Tim Mclelland collection)*

be attached to a centerline pylon designed with a 2,000lb load capacity. Although some references claimed that a 225 US gallon drop tank could be carried on this centerline pylon, it was in fact exclusively a weapons pylon and was not equipped for fuel transfer. Instead, it was configured to carry a single MK.12, Mk.28 or Mk.43 bomb, for medium or low-level "loft" (toss) delivery. The F-104C was equipped with an improved AN/ASG-14T-2 fire control system that replaced the F-104A's AN/ASG-14T-1. It made the F-104C capable of operating at night as well as in most daylight conditions, although the F-104C was not truly capable of all-weather operations. In addition to what would ostensibly be its main nuclear role, the aircraft was equipped to carry conventional bombs or rocket pods on wing and fuselage pylons. Likewise, the internal 20mm rotary cannon designed for the F-104A was retained, as well as the ability to carry a Sidewinder air-to-air missile on each wingtip. It was reported that the F-104C was not initially equipped with an internal cannon until the improved M61A1 version became available, but records confirm that the F-104C was equipped with the M61 from its first delivery to the USAF. The much-improved Starfighter promised to

deliver much more than its troubled predecessor, and one of the F-104A's most contentious deficiencies was overcome from the outset; the downward-firing escape system was replaced by Lockheed's C-2 upward-firing (rocket assisted) ejection seat.

The first F-104Cs began to reach TAC during September of 1958 (the first official delivery taking place on 16 October). Eventually the aircraft was assigned to four squadrons (434th, 435th, 436th, and 476th) of the 479th Tactical Fighter Wing based at George AFB in California and as planned, it was was primarily allocated to the nuclear strike role, but could also carry out ground attack missions with conventional weapons as required. In order to emphasise the capabilities of the new Starfighter variant, more record attempts were also organized and on 14 December 1959 an F-104C flown by Captain Joe B. Jordan boosted the world's altitude record to 103,395ft. This was the first time that an aircraft taking off under its own power had exceeded an altitude of 100,000ft and during this flight the aircraft also reached a speed of Mach 2.36, establishing a time-to-height record to 98,425ft of 15 minutes 4.92 seconds from brake release. Unlike the F-104A, the

F-104C's entry into USAF service was a more positive process and from October 1961 onwards, F-104Cs were assigned to Project Grindstone - an upgrade programme designed to provide the F-104C with greater capabilities. The most significant improvement was a new weapons pylon design that could be fitted under the fuselage, enabling a second pair of Sidewinder air-to-air missiles to be carried. The new Sidewinder stations were a useful bonus but in practice the idea proved to be unpopular, not least because the pylon produced a great deal of drag and the Sidewinder's glass seeker heads tended to become pitted by dust and debris kicked up by the aircraft's nose wheel. More importantly, the Sidewinder mountings blocked the centre pylon's function, meaning that a nuclear store couldn't be carried if the secondary Sidewinder pylons were fitted. However, Project Grindstone also endowed the F-104C with an additional capacity to carry 2.75in rockets, napalm bombs, and other devices including various free-fall weapons. This increased capability was soon put to use, and during the Cuban Missile Crisis in October 1962 the 479th TFW's F-104Cs were deployed to Key West in Florida, where they were prepared to

F-104A 56-0734 was assigned to Nasa for use as a high speed test research vehicle. During 1960 the aircraft was fitted with an instrumented nose cone containing thermocouples and various microphones, requiring the air data probe to be relocated to the port wing tip. Despite receiving Nasa's titles on its tail, the aircraft retained USAF titling for some time. *(Photo: Nasa)*

F-104A 56-0863 from the 157th FIS perfectly posted in front of the South Carolina Air National Guard's hangar at McEntire ANGB. The aircraft's fuselage is unpainted although the wings are sprayed gloss white, this being standard practice for the Starfighter. *(Photo: Tim McLelland collection)*

conduct air strikes against targets in Cuba, in anticipation of an invasion being ordered by the Whitehouse. Of course the crisis was resolved peacefully and the Starfighters returned to George AFB. It is not known whether the aircraft were to have carried nuclear weapons but given the F-104C's stated role, it seems more than likely that they would have.

The F-104C settled into service without the many problems that had affected the F-104A, although the new variant also had its share of difficulties. The main issue was the J79-GE-7 engine, and despite the improved reliability of this engine variant, more than 40 serious mishaps occurred over a five-year period, destroying 24 aircraft and killing nine pilots. This led to Project Seven Up, a modification programme undertaken by General Electric that began in May 1963 and ran until June 1964, effectively re-equipping the entire Starfighter fleet with new, even more reliable engines. The programme did make a significant contribution towards the F-104C's safety record, and by 1965 it was regarded as being no less reliable than other contemporary machines. This was a fortunate development, as within a matter of weeks the Starfighter went to war. During the early days of Operation Rolling Thunder in 1965, North Vietnamese fighter aircraft had became a significant problem for attacking USAF and US Navy strike aircraft. On April 3, 1965, three North Vietnamese Mig-17s attacked a strike

package near the Dong Phuong Thong Bridge, damaging a US Navy Crusader before escaping unscathed. The next day, two MiG-17s attacked a flight of four USAF F-105s and shot-down two of the aircraft. In order to meet this new threat, an EC-121D "College Eye" unit was assigned to the area, and TAC was tasked with the provision of F-104s to escort the EC-121s over the Gulf of Tonkin, providing defence against the MiGs for USAF strike aircraft operating in the region. During April 1965, a single squadron (the 476th TFS) of the 479th TFW deployed their F-104Cs to Kung Kuan Air Base in Taiwan, with aircraft rotated to the forward base at Da Nang Air Base in South Vietnam. Their mission was to fly MiG combat air patrol (MiGCAP) missions to protect American bombers - a task that was very different to the nuclear strike role for which the unit had trained, and for typical missions over Vietnam the aircraft was now armed with the single M61A1 20-mm cannon plus four AIM-9 Sidewinder air-to-air missiles. The effect of the F-104's deployment upon enemy MiG operations was immediate and dramatic. The MiG pilots soon learned to actively avoid contact with USAF strike packages that were being escorted by F-104s and during the entire deployment of the 476th only two fleeting encounters between F-104Cs and enemy fighters occurred. Given the Starfighter's inability to perform well as a close-in dogfighter, it is perhaps fortunate that the MiG pilots endowed the F-104 with

more respect than it probably deserved. As the MiG threat slowly abated, the 476th TFS was tasked with a wider variety of weather reconnaissance and ground attack missions. Some of these were against targets in North Vietnam, but most were close air-support missions against targets in the South under the direction of Forward Air Controllers. The F-104Cs were successful in this role, and the 476th TFS acquired a reputation for the provision of accurate cannon and bomb delivery, combined with rapid reaction times in response to immediate requests for air support. During this period, the 476th F-104Cs maintained a very impressive serviceability rate of 94.7 percent - a testament to both to the quality of the unit's maintenance personnel and to the greatly improved simplicity and maintainability of F-104C's systems.

The 476th TFS deployment to Vietnam wasn't without incident however. An F-104C was lost during a mission some 100nm SSW of DaNang on June 29 although the pilot was rescued with minor injuries. The 436th TFS assumed TAC's F-104C commitment in DaNang on 11 July, and began flying combat sorties the next day. Although a few MiGCAP missions were flown, the majority of the missions were now quick-reaction close-air support missions in support of ground troops. On 23 July, Capt. Roy Blakely attempted to crash-land his battle-damaged F-104C at Chu Lai. Blakely successfully settled

Manufactured in 1957, F-104A 56-0750 was assigned to the AFFTC at Edwards AFB, before being transferred to the 6512th Test Group, where it was redesignated as a JF-104A (Special Test aircraft in June 1962. Returning to the AFFTC as an F-104A in September 1964 it was retired to MASDC as FB0015 on 30 January 1968. *(Photo: Aeroplane)*

F-104A 56-0748 joined Nasa after serving with the AFFTC at Edwards AFB. This aircraft was also loaned to the US Navy for AIM-9B Sidewinder trials at NAF China Lake. It is one of only a few F-104A aircraft that still survives, and is currently on display at Dyess AFB in Texas. *(Photo: Tim Mclelland collection)*

The 479th Tactical Fighter Wing was perhaps the USAF's most significant operator of the Starfighter. The Wing took the Starfighter into combat in South East Asia and eventually became responsible for the training of some Nato pilots destined to fly the F-104G in Europe. The Wing's component Squadrons (the 434th, 435th, 436th and 476th Tactical Fighter Squadrons) each applied its own unit markings to their aircraft, although most were far less flamboyant than those applied to the Wing Commander's aircraft, and all unit markings were removed when aircraft were assigned to operations in support of the Berlin and Cuba crises. The 479th TFW was based at George AFB in California, and operated from October 1958 until late 1965.

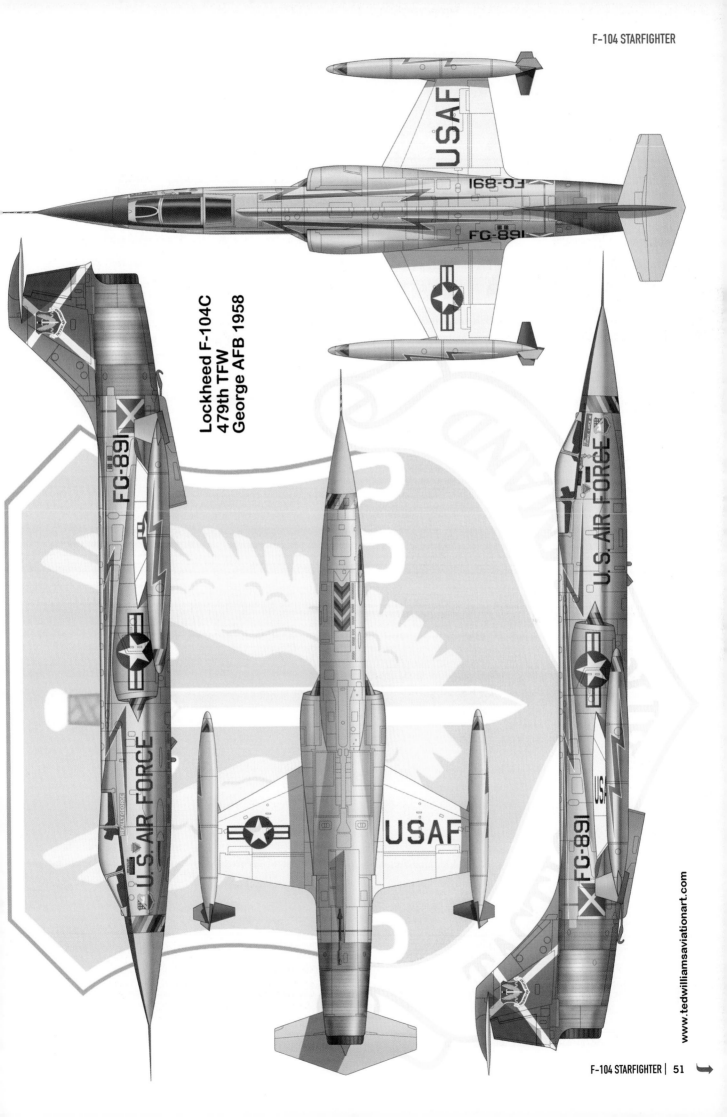

Lockheed F-104C
479th TFW
George AFB 1958

www.tedwilliamsaviationart.com

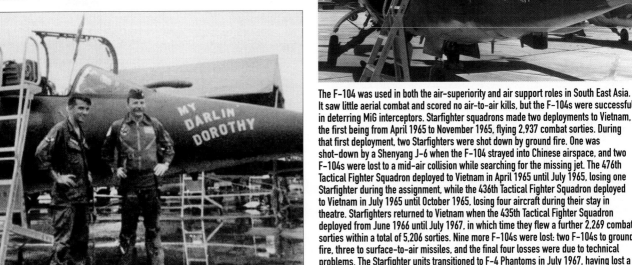

The F-104 was used in both the air-superiority and air support roles in South East Asia. It saw little aerial combat and scored no air-to-air kills, but the F-104s were successful in deterring MiG interceptors. Starfighter squadrons made two deployments to Vietnam, the first being from April 1965 to November 1965, flying 2,937 combat sorties. During that first deployment, two Starfighters were shot down by ground fire. One was shot-down by a Shenyang J-6 when the F-104 strayed into Chinese airspace, and two F-104s were lost to a mid-air collision while searching for the missing jet. The 476th Tactical Fighter Squadron deployed to Vietnam in April 1965 until July 1965, losing one Starfighter during the assignment, while the 436th Tactical Fighter Squadron deployed to Vietnam in July 1965 until October 1965, losing four aircraft during their stay in theatre. Starfighters returned to Vietnam when the 435th Tactical Fighter Squadron deployed from June 1966 until July 1967, in which time they flew a further 2,269 combat sorties within a total of 5,206 sorties. Nine more F-104s were lost: two F-104s to ground fire, three to surface-to-air missiles, and the final four losses were due to technical problems. The Starfighter units transitioned to F-4 Phantoms in July 1967, having lost a total of 14 F-104s during the conflict. After arrival in theatre, the Starfighters were soon camouflaged and many aircraft received individual pilot's artwork on their noses.
(Photos: USAF & Tim McLelland collection)

the aircraft onto the runway with the landing gear retracted, but the aircraft swerved off the runway into a sand dune and Blakeley was killed. The 436th TFS suffered another incident on 20 September 1965. F-104C pilot Major Philip E. Smith managed to become lost whilst flying an EC-121 escort mission over the Gulf of Tonkin. After several equipment failures and incorrect steering commands, he managed to stray over Hainan Island where he was shot down by a pair of Chinese MiG-19 (J-6) pilots (he ejected and was taken prisoner). While the rest of the squadron was busy looking for Major Smith, two other F-104 pilots lost sight of each other's aircraft and collided during their return to base. Thankfully, both pilots ejected and were recovered unharmed but only a week later another F-104C was shot down by enemy fire, and its pilot was killed. Following this series of incidents the remnants of the 435th went back to George AFB in November 1965 and F-4Cs Phantoms of the 390th TFS assumed the escort mission at DaNang. Although the F-104Cs had not shot down a single MiG aircraft during the deployment, their presence as escort aircraft had

undoubtedly diminished MiG activity to the point where MiGs were no longer considered as a primary threat to USAF aircraft flying missions over North Vietnam. But during the early months of 1966 the MiG threat began to re-emerge, when the supersonic MiG-21 began to appear. In response to this new threat the F-104C returned to Vietnam in June 1966, deployed to Udorn in Thailand. In the first deployment, eight F-104Cs from the 435th TFS deployed to Udorn on 6 June 1966. At the time of this second deployment to SEA, Tactical Air Command was already in the process of phasing-out the Starfighter, and the 479th TFW was already in the process of converting to the F-4 Phantom. Attached to PACAF's 8th TFW, an additional 12 F-104Cs joined the 8th TFW on 22 July. The 8th TFW F-104s were initially assigned to escort missions in support of F-105D strike aircraft against targets in North Vietnam. For most missions they were employed as escorts for the EF-105F Wild Weasel (engaged in defence suppression). Initially, the F-104Cs were not equipped with electronic countermeasures gear, and the Starfighter pilots had to rely on the F-105s for any warnings of enemy radar

lock-on dangers. As with the first deployment to the region, the presence of the F-104Cs managed to keep enemy MiGs away from the strike packages, although the Starfighter missions were often not without incident. On 1 August two F-104Cs were lost to enemy Surface-to-Air Missiles in just a single day, and TAC concluded that operating the F-104C in support of Wild Weasel missions was too risky to continue, chiefly because the F-104C's were not equipped with ECM gear. It was decided to withdraw the F-104C from support of strike missions over North Vietnam, although provision was made to return if the MiG threat reappeared. By late August, the F-104Cs were assigned to air strikes against targets in both Laos and South Vietnam, having switched from the Starfighter's design role of air superiority to TAC's primary role of ground attack. Losses during these missions were heavy, with three F-104s being downed by ground fire and SAMs over the next couple of months. The F-104C was of course less-than ideal for the ground attack role, being incapable of carrying an adequately large conventional offensive load (it's main armament had in

effect been a single nuclear bomb). In addition, it could not carry out operations in the kind of weather conditions that normally prevailed in the region, nor could it sustain a lot of battle damage. By late 1966, all F-104s in Southeast Asia had received APR-25/26 RHAW gear under Project Pronto, and they resumed flying escort missions over North Vietnam. The Starfighter took part in Operation Bolo on 2 January 1967, the famous USAF attempt to lure North Vietnamese fighters into aerial combat. Not surprisingly, the F-104s were not used to actively entice and engage MiG pilots, but they were used instead to protect the egressing F-4 Phantom force. As more and more Phantoms began to reach the region, TAC decided to replace these F-104Cs by the more efficient F-4D in July 1967. The 435th was then re-established at George AFB for the last time. With operational duties at an end, TAC withdrew the F-104C and the surviving examples were mostly transferred to the 198th TFS of the Puerto Rico Air National Guard where they replaced that unit's elderly F-86H Sabre fighter-bombers. They remained active with the 198th TFS until

July 1975 when they were finally replaced by A-7 Corsairs. The Starfighter had played an important role during the Vietnam War, even if it was not responsible for any direct MiG losses. The aircraft's presence had been sufficient to deter a great deal of MiG activity, and as a ground attack platform the aircraft had performed surprisingly well, despite having been designed for a completely different environment. But TAC's almost reluctant acceptance of the Starfighter had been a relatively fleeting relationship, and in January 1967 Defense Secretary Robert McNamara announced that the last remaining operational Starfighters would be removed from USAF service early in 1968. This could well have been a premature end to the Starfighter's history, but of course it was in many respects only the beginning.

The Starfighter's phenomenal success as a multi-role warplane is a story of commercial defeat being turned into victory. The F-104A had been a clear disappointment for Lockheed, having been hampered by a variety of technical problems that had plagued its entry into service. The J79 engine that had been chosen for the aircraft was a

logical choice, but the Starfighter's development continually progressed beyond the rate at which the J79 was developed, and it was the engine's unreliability that caused so many of the F-104A's problems. Of course there were other issues too, not least the aircraft's impractical escape system, but also the aircraft's very demanding handling characteristics. Although Kelly Johnson and his team had deliberately set out to produce an aircraft that was easy to handle and operate, but the requirements for high speed and altitude performance inevitably meant that the aircraft would be less suited to lower speeds. The result was an aircraft that required skillful handling when it was outside of its operational environment, particularly during take-off and landing, when speed had to be kept relatively high in order to compensate for the aircraft's extremely small wings that provided a meager amount of lift. The ingenious BLC system artificially lowered the aircraft's landing speed and helped to keep the aircraft's approach speed within a more acceptable range, but it relied on engine power to provide the necessary high-pressure air. The system worked well,

JF-104A 56-0749 on the ramp at the NASA Flight Research Center (now the Dryden Flight Research Center) at Edwards AFB. The aircraft is shown with the Air Launched Sounding Rocket (ALSOR) attached to the underside. NASA test pilot Milton O. Thompson ejected from this aircraft on 20 December 1962, after an asymmetrical flap condition made the jet uncontrollable. *(Photo: Nasa)*

Four Starfighters from the Air Force Flight Test Center, based at Edwards AFB during the 1960s. 56–0772 was the 43rd F–104A to be built, while 56–0766 went on the serve with the 4760th Crew Training Squadron at Webb AFB. *(Photo: USAF)*

but if there was any problem with the engine (as there often was) then the BLC system was useless and the Starfighter's tiny wings could barely provide sufficient lift to keep the aircraft airborne. The result was an aircraft that required extremely careful handling particularly during the landing phase when the Starfighter literally had to be flown down to the runway rather than being allowed to sink onto it. It was a demanding aeroplane that required the pilot's constant attention, and even without any technical problems, the F-104A was by no means an aircraft for the inexperienced. The situation improved significantly with the arrival of the F-104C, and this variant's better engine and improved escape system created an aircraft that was at least technically sound, even if it still suffered from the same handling issues.

The Starfighter was a victim not only of developmental and design problems, but also of confused defence procurement thinking. By the time that the F-104A was ready for service, Tactical Air Command had lost interest in it, largely because other more suitable designs were under development. By comparison, Air Defense Command enjoyed a good relationship with the aircraft but the aircraft was destined to compete with other

emerging designs that offered different (and often better) solutions to the requirements of both TAC and ADC. When Tactical Air Command did eventually agree to acquire a small fleet of Starfighters, the aircraft was regarded as a stopgap until something better came along. The fact that they eventually proved to be immensely useful fighter-bombers that were in place at the very time that they were needed (for the Vietnam War) was perhaps a case of good luck. But even after the Vietnam deployments, the Starfighter's story was still undoubtedly a disappointing one. Kelly Johnson and his team had created an outstanding machine that did everything they had hoped for and much more, but by the time that it was completed, military thinking had moved on and technology had advanced to such a stage where a high speed "daylight point interceptor" (which is what the F-104A really was) had become largely irrelevant to the USAF's requirements. However, coincidence once again played an important part in the Starfighter's history, and far away across the Atlantic, Nato's European air arms were looking for a new aircraft to fill an emerging requirement for an aircraft capable of performing a variety of roles, most notably

the delivery of American B-43 tactical nuclear bombs. Germany was the main potential customer although many other countries were also looking towards a replacement for elderly F-86 Sabre and F-84 Thunderstreaks. Indeed, only Britain and France seemed to be excluded from this process, having opted to pursue their own indigenous designs in the shape of the Lightning, Buccaneer and Mirage. Both the US Government and Lockheed estimated that the Nato requirement promised a potential market for more than 2,000 aircraft and it was hardly surprising that Lockheed was extremely keen to secure its part in what eventually became known as the Sale of the Century. Rather more surprising was that the Starfighter emerged as the chosen design.

Strenuous efforts were made by a variety of aerospace companies to convince the customer countries that various aircraft types would be ideal for the new fighter-bomber requirements that were being identified, although the main emphasis was on Germany, where the largest market would be. Britain made some effort to sell the Buccaneer and Lighting to Germany but by any standards the British Government's attitude was indifferent, even if English

The USAF temporarily assigned a number of F-104As to the US Navy for trials with the (then) new AIM-9 Sidewinder air-to-air missile. Deployed to Naval Weapons Center at NAF China Lake, F-104A 56-0757 crashed on take-off on 7 April 1961 just off the runway at George AFB on a return flight to China Lake during Sidewinder missile tests. Pilot U.S. Marine Corp Capt. David Hess was killed, the cause later found to be a failure of flight line personnel to activate circuit breakers, which prevented the afterburner from engaging. The take-off had been attempted with a tail wind and the aircraft failed to achieve sufficient take-off speed. On 22September 1960, US Marine Corps Captain Howard Casada Jr. was killed when his Starfighter (56-0740) crashed into the southern face of Josephine Peak, the cause being a suspected pilot loss of consciousness due to oxygen supply failure at altitude. *(Photos: USAF)*

The Starfighter's impressive speed and altitude performance led to a decision to use the aircraft to train test pilots destined to fly the rocket-powered X-15. The concept of using the F-104 as a "manned spacecraft transition trainer" is credited to astronaut Frank Borman who was both a student and instructor at the Air Force's Aerospace Research Pilot School. The basic Starfighter airframe was modified to accommodate a 6,000lb thrust rocket engine at the base of the vertical tail, reaction control thrusters in the nose and in each wing tip, increased wing span, tanks to store the rocket propellants, provision for a full pressure suit, a cockpit hand controller to operate the reaction control thrusters, and modified cockpit instrumentation. The NF-104 was developed in 1963 and the aircraft proved itself capable of a zoom climb to more than 100,000ft, where the pilot could experience zero g, and use reaction controls to handle the aircraft. Only 35 students flew the NF-104 and after five preparation flights in a standard dual-control Starfighter, the students performed the two high-altitude NF-104 sorties. Take-off was achieved with normal jet power, and after a climb to 30-40,000 feet, the aircraft was accelerated to Mach 1.9. The pilot then ignited the rocket engine and pitched the nose up to start the steep climb. After two minutes the Starfighter passed through 80,000 feet, the jet engine cut out, and the pilot began a parabolic arc to the peak altitude. Once back to a lower altitude, the pilot restarted the jet engine and made a conventional landing, the whole mission lasted approximately 35 minutes. One NF-104 was destroyed on 10 December 1963 when Colonel Chuck Yeager attempted to reach an altitude record, but at 104,000ft the aircraft entered an uncontrollable yaw and rolling motion. Yeager was forced to eject at 11,000 feet (the story was depicted in the book and movie "The Right Stuff"). Although many accidents occurred during the NF-104 programme, the aircraft provided the USAF and Nasa with valuable astronaut training and the surviving pair of NF-104s remained in use until December 1971, by which stage the USAF's requirement for astronaut training had been transferred to Nasa. The NF-104A achieved an unofficial record height of 118,860ft on 6 December 1963 in the hands of Major Robert Smith. *(Photos: USAF)*

Electric and Blackburn's were rather more serious. The proposed Saunders-Roe 177 also became a serious contender for some time, but it soon became clear that they were competing against much stronger candidates from the USA. The Vought F-8 Crusader and Republic F-105 Thunderchief were proposed, as were versions of the Grumman Tiger, but Lockheed assembled a new proposal for an improved version of the Starfighter, and much to the astonishment of media and many military officials, it was this project that soon captured Germany's interest. It seemed like a remarkable development when the Starfighter seemed to be the least-appropriate aircraft on offer, with a troubled USAF service record, a poor accident rate, and performance figures that were still unproven (Lockheed's proposed Starfighter export derivative had yet to be built). Most importantly, the F-104 was an interceptor, not an attack platform. It was only years later that the likely reason for Lockheed's sales triumph became clear, when news of commercial bribery scandals began to hit the news headlines. The whole story of how some of Lockheed's officials attempted to influence Germany and the Netherlands (plus other countries too) is a complicated and contentious one, but few observers now doubt that even though the Starfighter was an impressive design, it was probably chosen by Germany because of some dubious commercial deals that were completed in

secret. Lockheed's public assertion was that the aircraft was chosen on merit, the final decision having been made after a fly-off competition between an F-104C and a Grumman F11F Tiger. The F-104 reportedly landed in a shorter distance (by some 455ft) and during a simultaneous climb to 50,000ft the Starfighter attained this height in just under four minutes, while the Tiger was still struggling to exceed 35,000ft two minutes later. This kind of performance comparison must have influenced Germany (and others), but Germany required a truly multi-role aircraft that could perform both defence and attack roles, and this prompted Lockheed to develop the F-104G (the 'G' denoting Germany, although the new variant was created with all of Nato in mind). The F-104G (Lockheed Model 683-10-19) was externally similar to the earlier F-104C day fighter, but it differed in being a multi-role, all-weather aircraft rather than ostensibly being a fighter (despite being designated as fighters, TAC's F-104Cs had of course already been operated as strike aircraft). The F-104G had a full all-weather capability, and was fitted with an Autonetics F15A-41B NASARR (North American Search and Ranging Radar) fire control system. The fire control system was optimized in two basic air-to-ground and air-to-air modes, these being for bombing and navigation or target interception. In the air-to-air mode, it provided radar search, acquisition and automatic tracking of aerial

targets to enable collision-course attacks with automatic missile release, acting in conjunction with a director-type gun sight for the M-61 Vulcan cannon. The director gun sight gave the pilot an optical line-of-sight indication after the NASARR had computed the required lead angle. The weapons sight incorporated a basic infrared facility with common optics developed by Lockheed, which gave the aircraft some night-sighting capability. For air-to-ground modes, the NASAAR provided the pilot with range information for visual bombing computation, ground mapping for all-weather bombing and navigation, contour mapping for navigation, and terrain avoidance for low-level combat missions (the caged sight could also be used as an aiming reference for visual dive-bombing). The F-104G was also equipped with a Litton LN-3 inertial navigator that provided the pilot with continuous optical indication of direction and distance to a preselected target (the F-104G was one or the first combat aircraft to make use of such a system) however the LN-3 was to encounter major development problems and it failed to perform satisfactorily for some time.

The fuselage and flying surface structures were strengthened to enable the aircraft to carry an increased offensive weapons load and to handle the stresses of low-altitude combat missions flown at high speeds. Some 36 new forgings were needed to reinforce the fuselage mainframes, wing fittings and

YF-104A 55-2961 was modified to test a Reaction Control System that had been introduced in the X-1B rocket vehicle. Following the discovery of fuel tank cracks, the X-1B was grounded and the F-104 was selected as a suitable replacement, necessary to support the X-15 programme. The hydrogen peroxide RCS was installed with vents in the aircraft's nose and wing tips. Some 28 flights were flown with the system and during these tests the aircraft reached 83,000ft and the results of these tests were used for further development of the X-15.

beams, fuselage longerons, joints, and tail frames, tail beams and ribs, plus some new fuselage skins. Reinforcements were also made to the trailing-edge flap fittings to allow partial deflections of up to 15 degrees during combat manoeuvres, allowing reductions of up to 33 percent in turning radius at altitudes of 5,000 feet – a useful improvement for an aircraft that suffered from relatively poor turning performance.

The F-104G incorporated the same seven weapons stations that had been fitted to the F-104C. One was positioned on the fuselage centreline (primarily for the carriage of a single nuclear store), one under each wing, and one at each wing tip, and this enabled up to 4,000lb of external stores to be carried. The internal fuel capacity was increased from 1,624 to 1,784 US gallons. In overall terms the proportions of the F-104G airframe remained unchanged although the new "Super Starfighter" differed from its predecessor in that it incorporated a slightly larger tail fin design that had first been designed for the twin-seat dual-control trainer version of the F-104A/C. The great fin and rudder area provided a considerable improvement in longitudinal stability at high Mach numbers, and with a new fully powered rudder, the aircraft had much better directional control and was no longer prone to "snaking" in some conditions. The revised tail configuration became standard for this and all subsequent Starfighters that were manufactured. The

stabilator (combined elevator and tailplane) servo mechanism was modified to afford increased hinge movement as demanded by the increased control power required by low-altitude operations at increased gross weights, and the amount of power for the control system booster was increased. The hinge and operating controls were contained within the empennage contours, to avoid external fairings. With these new improvements the F-104G had a higher maximum take-off weight compared to the F-104C and in order to cope with the extra weight and the correspondingly higher landing speeds, larger wheels were fitted with new brakes that were fully powered and equipped with anti-skid capability. Additionally, the ribbon tail braking parachute was increased in diameter from 16ft to 18ft. Lockheed's C-2 rocket-boosted upward-firing ejector seat was selected as standard for the F-104G, and it was cleared for use at all altitudes down to ground level at speeds between 90 knots and 550 knots, thereby ensuring that the pilot had a viable means of escape in any stage of the Starfighter's flight regime. General Electric's J79-GE-11A was adopted for the F-104G, rated at 10,000lb (15,600lb with reheat). The J79 engines were to be produced under license in Europe, and eventually arrangements were made for manufacture by MAN-Turbo in Germany, by the Fabrique Nationale in Belgium, or by Fiat in Italy.

F-104A-15-LO (serial number 56-0770) was modified by Lockheed to become the aerodynamic prototype of the F-104G, although it was only an aerodynamic prototype, lacking the internal airframe strengthening and many of the internal systems of the definitive F-104G. It flew for the first time at Palmdale on 1 September 1960. The first new-build F-104G (Werke Number 2001) was flown for the first time on 5 October 1960, and this became the first of the initial German order for 66 examples, with production deliveries starting in May of 1961. The German order was secured in 1958 when Federal Defence Minister Franz Josef Strauss announced (on 6 November) that the F-104G would be the preferred aircraft for Germany's interceptor, fighter-bomber and reconnaissance needs. The initial contract for 66 aircraft (issued on 18 March 1959) was later increased to 96 plus 30 dual control trainers. Agreement was eventually made for Germany to produce 210 examples and to purchase a further 364 from joint co-operation with other European companies, increasing overall procurement to 670 airframes.

European production sites were clustered into four groups, based on geographical location. The South Group comprised Dornier at Munich, Heinkel at Speyer, Messerschmitt at Augsburg (later reorganized as Messerschmitt-Bolkow-Blohm, or MBB), and Siebel at Donauworth, plus BMW at Koblenz

for J79 engine production. The North Group included the Dutch companies Fokker at Schipol plus Dordrech and Aviolanda at Papendrecht, together with the German companies Focke Wulf at Bremen, Hamburger Flugzeugbau in Hamburg and Weserflugzeugbau at Einswarden. The West Group consisted of SABCA (Societe Anonyme Belge de Constructions Aeronautiques) and Fairey SA of Belgium, where a joint facility was established at Gosselies near Charleroi, with Fabrique Nationale in Brussels handling J79 production. The Italian Group consisted of Fiat at Turin as the prime contractor, with Aerfer-Macchi, Piaggio, SACA, and SIAI-Marchetti as subcontractors. Canadair in Canada was contracted to supply 121 sets of wings, aft fuselage, and tail assemblies to Germany and the Netherlands, plus an additional 40 sets to the original manufacturer in California. Lockheed remained involved in the license production programmes, and supplied small numbers of complete F-104Gs along with knock-down kits of parts to the customer countries, in order to assist in the launch of their own individual programmess. Lockheed also built the first 66 F-104Gs for the Luftwaffe and an additional 84 aircraft for USAF Mutual Aid contracts. The initial production schedule specified 210 aircraft to be built by the South Group, 350 by the North Group, 188 by the West Group, and 199 by the Italian group. Plans were put in place to share production components between sites and even complete airplanes were eventually distributed between the various Groups so that each country's aircraft didn't necessarily

all come from the same source. Germany's programme illustrated this process clearly, with the Luftwaffe eventually receiving 700 F-104Gs that came from no less than five different nations. Lockheed eventually constructed 139 F-104Gs, which were delivered to the air forces of Germany, Greece, Norway, and Turkey, together with pattern aircraft that were delivered to the manufacturers in Belgium and Italy. Lockheed also assumed primary responsibility for the production of TF-104G combat trainers. The South Group's first F-104G completed its maiden flight on 5 October 1960 and this group eventually built 210 aircraft, all of them destined for West Germany's Luftwaffe. The West Group's first F-104G flew for the first time on 3 August 1961, with ensuing production examples going both to the Force Aerienne Belge and to the Luftwaffe. The North Group's first F-104G took to the air on 11

November 1961 and some 231 aircraft were eventually built for both the Koninklijke Luchtmacht (Royal Netherlands Air Force) and the Luftwaffe. The Italian Group saw its first Starfighter take to the skies on 9 June 1962, and production of 169 aircraft followed, for Dutch, German, and Italian orders. Once the European F-104G program was well underway, the USAF ordered 140 F-104Gs to be built by Canadair for various NATO nations as part of MAP arrangements. These were intended for Norway, Denmark, Greece, Turkey, and Spain and followed Canadian-built CF-104s (destined for the RCAF) off the production line. Canadair's F-104Gs were essentially similar to European-built aircraft, other than in terms of the NASARR that was installed. The first of the Canadair-built F-104Gs for Europe (6001, with USAF serial number 62-12302) made its first flight on 30 July 1963, and deliveries began a few weeks later. ❖

The QF-104A was a modified version of the F-104A, designed to be flown remotely by pilots on the ground or inside an accompanying aircraft. The conversion programme was approved on 19 February 1960 for the creation of unmanned high altitude, high speed targets for the development of ground-to-air (BOMARC) and air-to-air (AIM-7, AIM-9, GAR-2B, MB-1 and AIM-4) missiles. It is believed that 22 aircraft were ultimately delivered to the USAF, all being former F-104A aircraft. The recorded airframes were:– YF-104A 55-2957, 55-2963, 55-2965, 55-2966, 55-2968, 56-2969, 55-2971. F-104A 56-730, 56-734, 56-735, 56-736, 56-737, 56-739, 56-741, 56-743, 56-745, 56-746, 56-747, 56-796, 56-836. Externally similar to the F-104A, the QF-104A received anti-skid brakes, a smoke generator system (fuel pumped into the engine exhaust), remote control equipment, an in-flight engine starting system, a self-destruction device, additional internal fuel, and an optional camera recording system. Most notably, the aircraft were painted in high visibility fluorescent orange paint. *(Photos: Lockheed)*

THE F-104 STARFIGHTER IN DETAIL

Nasa's F-104G N826NA was the last Starfighter to be operated by the agency. The last flight occurred on 3 February 1994 by which stage the former Luftwaffe aircraft had completed 1,425 flights. The aircraft therefore earned the distinction of being the very last Starfighter to operate in US Governmental service. It is now on permanent display at Edwards AFB near the Dryden research facility. *(Photo: Nasa)*

F-104A internal layout

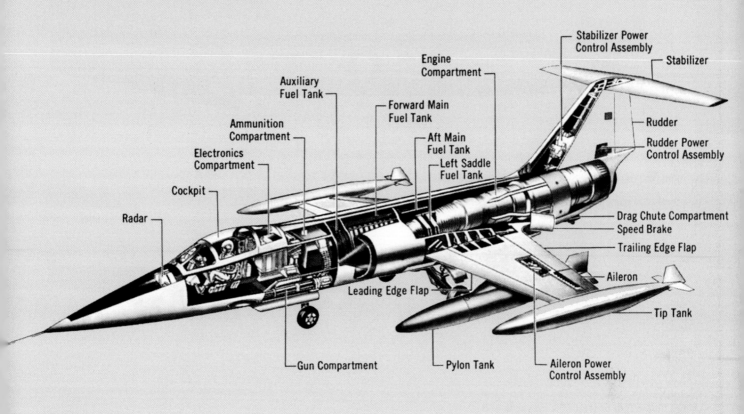

Stabilizer Power Control Assembly

Stabilizer

Engine Compartment

Auxiliary Fuel Tank

Forward Main Fuel Tank

Ammunition Compartment

Aft Main Fuel Tank

Left Saddle Fuel Tank

Electronics Compartment

Cockpit

Rudder

Rudder Power Control Assembly

Radar

Drag Chute Compartment
Speed Brake

Trailing Edge Flap

Aileron

Leading Edge Flap

Tip Tank

Gun Compartment

Pylon Tank

Aileron Power Control Assembly

F-104A internal layout
(engine, fuel and avionics)

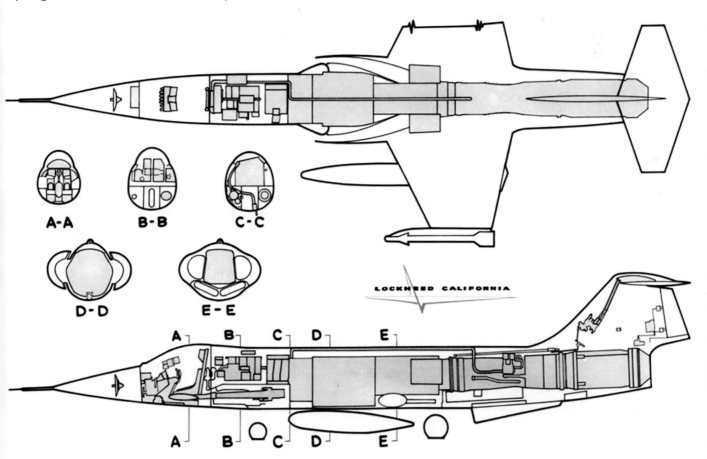

A-A   B-B   C-C

D-D   E-E

LOCKHEED CALIFORNIA

A   B   C   D   E

A   B   C   D   E

F-104A
No.9 Squadron, Pakistan Air Force
Unpainted fuselage with white wings. National insignia in green and white.

F-104A
National Aeronautics & Space Administration
Edwards AFB
Two-tone blue paint scheme with white wings and upper fuselage (yellow trim).
Nasa logo on intake.

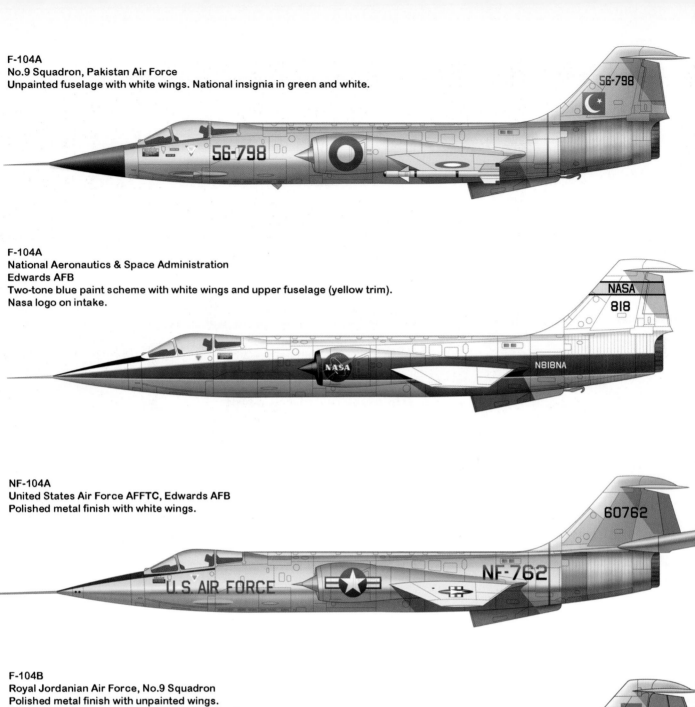

NF-104A
United States Air Force AFFTC, Edwards AFB
Polished metal finish with white wings.

F-104B
Royal Jordanian Air Force, No.9 Squadron
Polished metal finish with unpainted wings.
National insignia in green, black, white and red.

F-104C
United States Air Force, 479th Tactical Fighter WIng
Polished metal finish with white wings. Unit insignia in red and white.

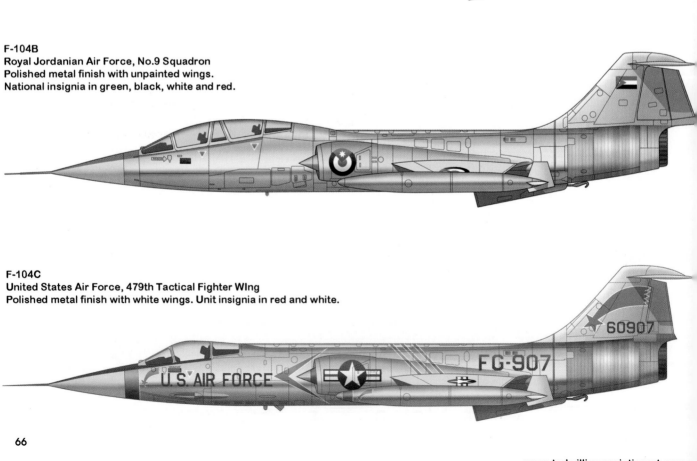

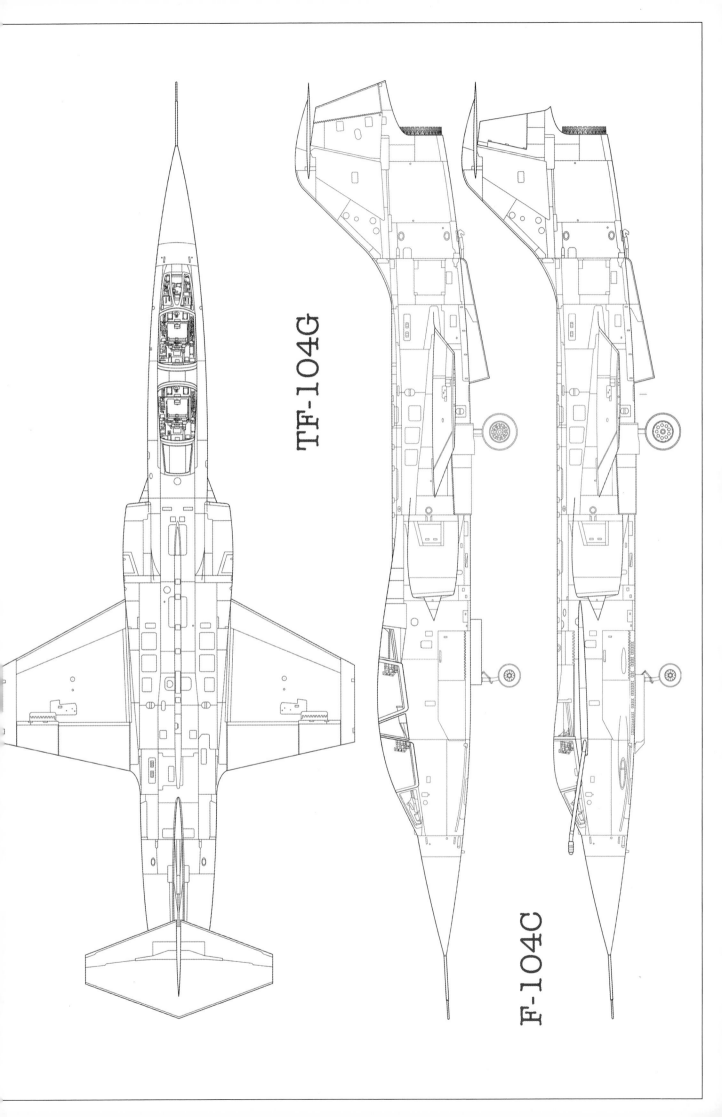

TF-104G

F-104C

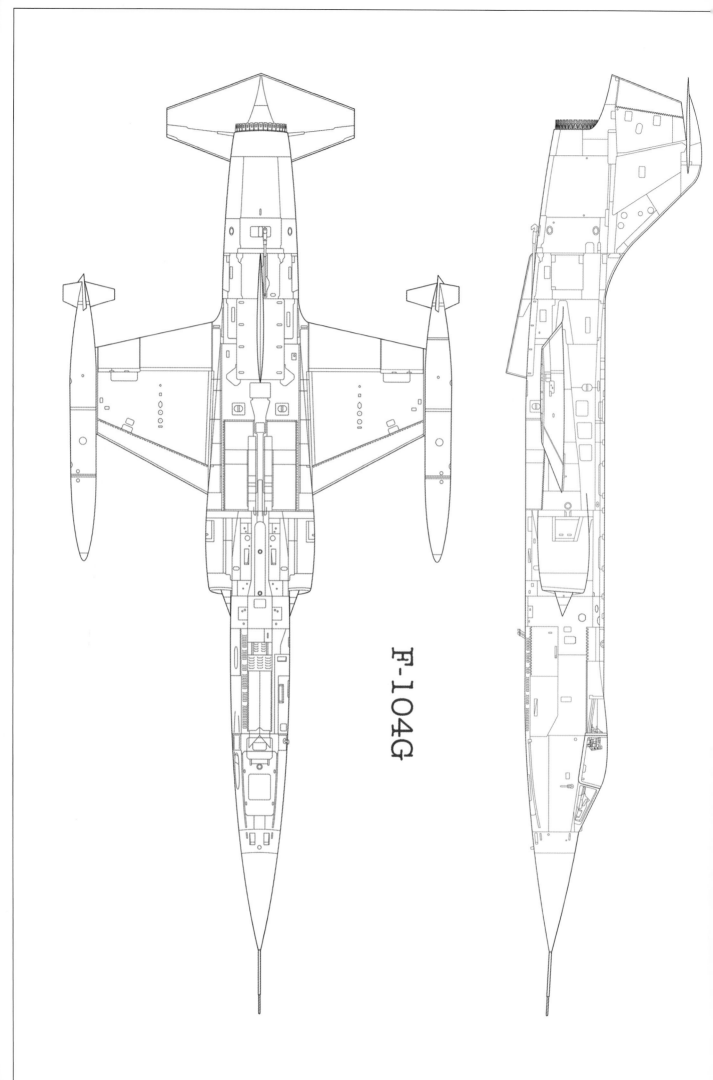

F-104G

Lockheed F-104 Starfighter

F-104G

F-104G

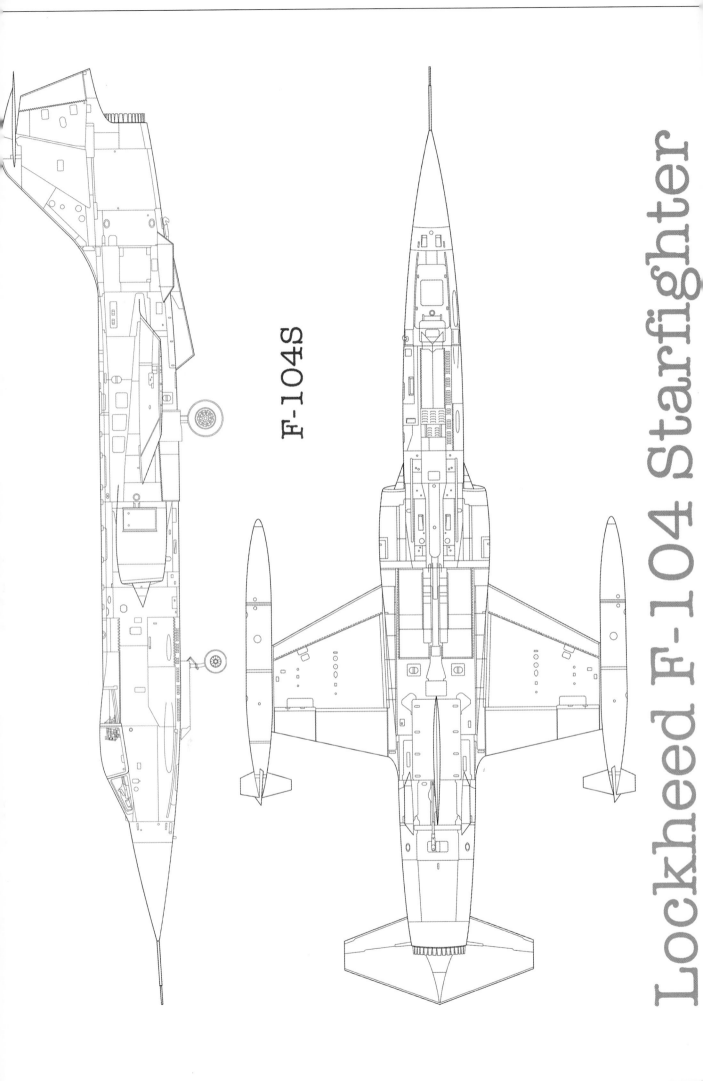

F-104S

Lockheed F-104 Starfighter

04C
ited States Air Force, 479th Tactical Fighter Wing
ployed to Udorn AB, Thailand
Asia camouflage with "Smoke II" markings on nose.

04DJ
pan Air Self Defense Force, No.202 Squadron
painted fuselage with white wings. Red and white exercise markings.
it markings on tail, in yellow and orange

104D
ited States Air Force, 198th Tactical Fighter Squadron
erto Rico Air National Guard
Asia camouflage with ANG badge on tail.

104G
rce Aerienne Belgique, No.31 Squadron, 10th Wing
Asia-style camouflage with black/yellow tip tank (Tiger Meet markings)

104G
oyal Danish Air Force, Esk.723
verall green finish with reduced-size national insignia and unit badge
ose cone painted medium green.

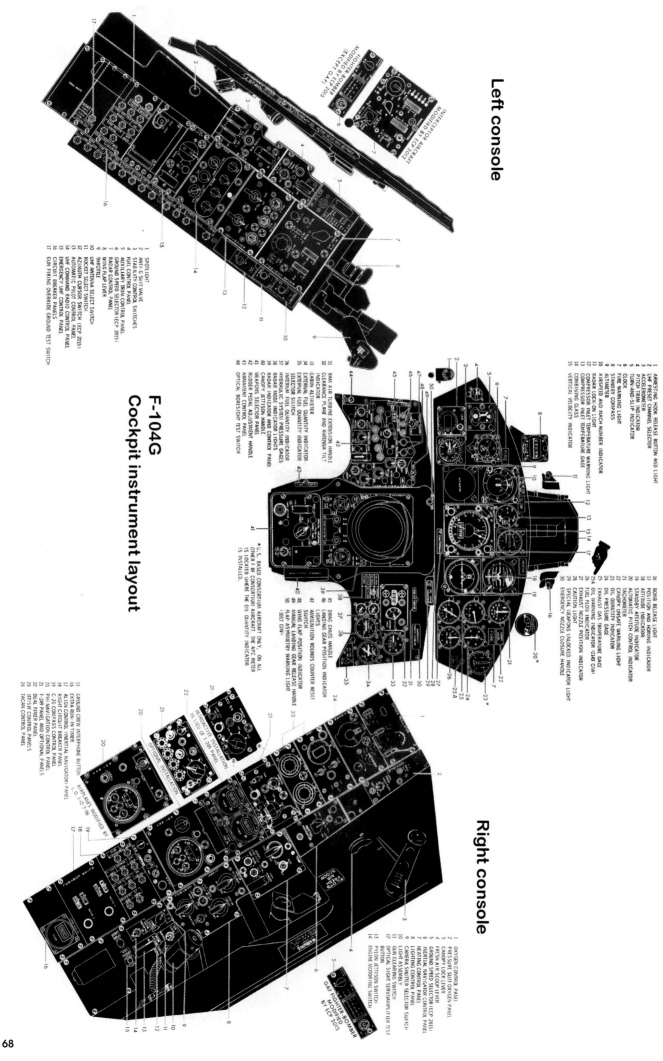

Left console

1 SPOTLIGHT
2 ANTI-G SUIT VALVE
3 STABILITY CONTROL SWITCHES
4 FUEL CONTROL PANEL
5 AUXILIARY TRIM CONTROL SWITCHES
6 GROUND SPEED SELECTOR (ECP 2015)
7 RADAR CONTROL PANEL
8 WING FLAP LEVER
9 THROTTLE
10 UHF ANTENNA SELECT SWITCH
11 ROCKET SELECT SWITCH (ECP 2015)
12 AZIMUTH CURSOR SWITCH
13 AUTOMATIC PILOT CONTROL PANEL
14 UHF COMMAND RADIO CONTROL PANEL
15 EMERGENCY UHF CONTROL PANEL
16 CIRCUIT BREAKER PANELS
17 GUN FIRING OVERRIDE GROUND TEST SWITCH

F-104G
Cockpit instrument layout

1 ARRESTING HOOK RELEASE BUTTON AND LIGHT
2 UHF PRESET CHANNEL SELECTOR
3 ACCELEROMETER
4 PITCH TRIM INDICATOR
5 TURN-AND-SLIP INDICATOR
6 CLOCK
7 TACHOMETER
8 STANDBY COMPASS
9 FIRE WARNING LIGHT
10 ALTIMETER
11 RADAR LOCK-ON LIGHT
12 AIRSPEED AND MACH NUMBER INDICATOR
13 COMPRESSOR INLET TEMPERATURE WARNING LIGHT
14 COMPRESSOR INLET TEMPERATURE GAGE
15 COMBINING GLASS
VERTICAL VELOCITY INDICATOR

16 OXYGEN CONTROL PANEL
17 POSITION AND HOMING INDICATOR
18 ATTITUDE INDICATOR
19 STANDBY ATTITUDE INDICATOR
20 AUTOMATIC PITCH CONTROL INDICATOR
21 TACHOMETER
22 CANOPY UNSAFE WARNING LIGHT
23 OIL QUANTITY INDICATOR
24 OIL PRESSURE GAGE
25 EXHAUST GAS TEMPERATURE GAGE
25A OIL WARNING INDICATOR (248 CIV)
26 FUEL FLOW INDICATOR
27 EXHAUST NOZZLE POSITION INDICATOR
28 CAUTION LIGHT
29 SPECIAL WEAPONS UNLOCKED INDICATOR LIGHT
30 EMERGENCY NOZZLE CLOSURE HANDLE

31 RAM AIR TURBINE EXTENSION HANDLE
32 CLEARANCE PLANE AND ANTENNA TILT INDICATOR
33 CABIN ALTIMETER
34 EXTERNAL FUEL QUANTITY INDICATOR
35 INTERNAL FUEL QUANTITY INDICATOR
36 SELECTOR SWITCH
37 HYDRAULIC SYSTEM PRESSURE GAGES
38 RADAR MODE INDICATOR LIGHTS
39 RADAR INDICATOR AND CONTROL PANEL
40 CANOPY JETTISON HANDLE
41 WEAPONS SELECTOR PANEL
42 RUDDER PEDAL ADJUSTMENT HANDLE
43 ARMAMENT CONTROL PANEL
44 OPTICAL BORESIGHT TEST SWITCH

35 DRAG CHUTE HANDLE
36 LANDING GEAR POSITION INDICATOR
37 FIRE
38 AMMUNITION ROUNDS COUNTER RESET
47 WING FLAP POSITION INDICATOR
48 AMMUNITION ROUNDS COUNTER
49 MANUAL LANDING GEAR RELEASE HANDLE
50 FLAP ASYMMETRY WARNING LIGHT
IDLT CPU

* U.S. BASED CONSORTIUM AIRCAFT ONLY. ON ALL OTHER F-104 CONSORTIUM AIRCRAFT THE APC METER IS LOCATED WHERE THE OIL QUANTITY INDICATOR IS INSTALLED.

Right console

1 OXYGEN CONTROL PANEL
2 PRESSURE SUIT OXYGEN PANEL
3 FRESH AIR SCOOP LEVER
4 CANOPY LOCK LEVER
5 GROUND SPEED SELECTOR (ECP 2015)
6 INERTIAL NAVIGATOR CONTROL PANEL
7 HEATING CONTROL PANEL
8 LIGHTING CONTROL PANEL
9 LIGHT ASSEMBLY
10 CAMERA SHUTTER SELECTOR SWITCH
11 GUN CLEARING SWITCH
12 OPTICAL SIGHT SERVOAMPLIFIER TEST BUTTON
13 PYLON JETTISON SWITCH
14 ENGINE MOTORING SWITCH

15 GROUND CREW INTERPHONE BUTTON
16 EXTRA RUN-IN TIMER
17 RIGHT CIRCUIT BREAKER PANEL
18 ALIGN CONTROL PANEL
19 C-2G COMPASS CONTROL PANEL
20 PHI NAVIGATION CONTROL PANEL
21 T-2A PANEL AND OPTIONAL PANELS
22 DUAL TIMER PANEL
23 IFF/SIF CONTROL PANELS
24 TACAN CONTROL PANEL

RETROFICIVE INSTALLATION IN LIEU OF T-2A PANEL
OPTIONAL INSTALLATION
AIRPLANES MODIFIED BY I.O. 1-C-706

68

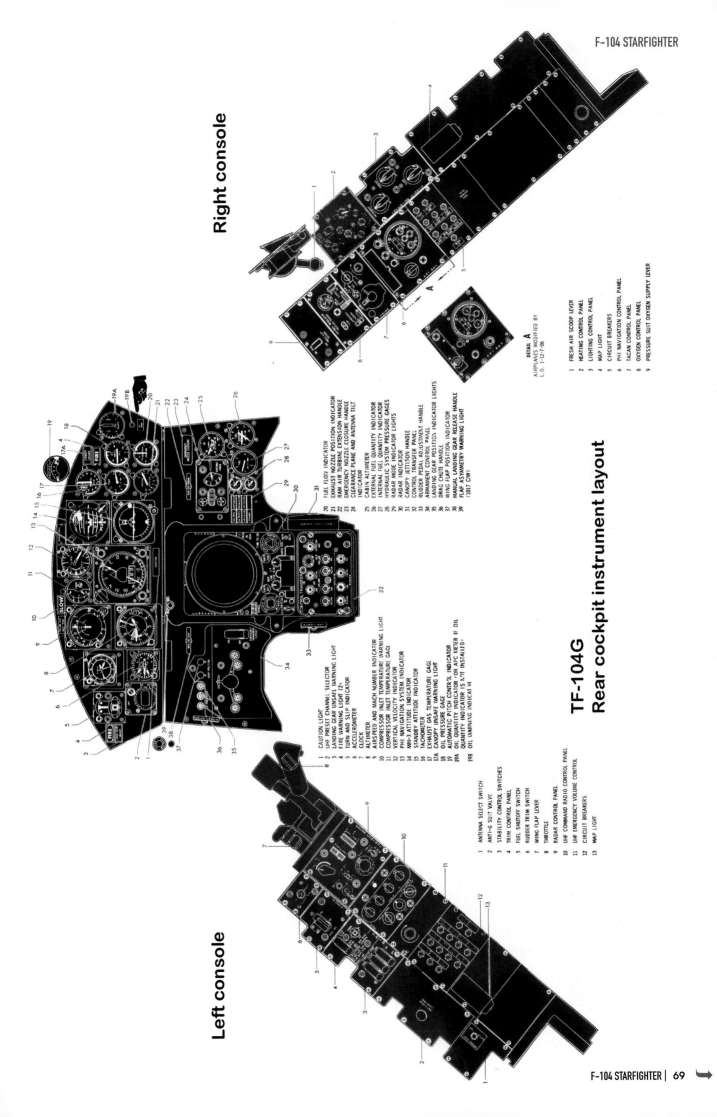

Right console

Left console

TF-104G
Rear cockpit instrument layout

DETAIL A
AIRPLANES MODIFIED BY
L.O. 1-12-7-06

1 FRESH AIR SCOOP LEVER
2 HEATING CONTROL PANEL
3 LIGHTING CONTROL PANEL
4 MAP LIGHT
5 CIRCUIT BREAKERS
6 PHI NAVIGATION CONTROL PANEL
7 TACAN CONTROL PANEL
8 OXYGEN CONTROL PANEL
9 PRESSURE SUIT OXYGEN SUPPLY LEVER

1 CAUTION LIGHT
2 UHF PRESET CHANNEL SELECTOR
3 LANDING GEAR UNSAFE WARNING LIGHT
4 FIRE WARNING LIGHT (2)
5 TURN AND SLIP INDICATOR
6 ACCELEROMETER
7 CLOCK
8 ALTIMETER
9 AIRSPEED AND MACH NUMBER INDICATOR
10 COMPRESSOR INLET TEMPERATURE WARNING LIGHT
11 COMPRESSOR INLET TEMPERATURE GAGE
12 VERTICAL VELOCITY INDICATOR
13 PHI NAVIGATION SYSTEM INDICATOR
14 MM-3 ATTITUDE INDICATOR
15 STANDBY ATTITUDE INDICATOR
16 TACHOMETER
17 EXHAUST GAS TEMPERATURE GAGE
17A CANOPY UNSAFE WARNING LIGHT
18 OIL PRESSURE GAGE
19 AUTOMATIC PITCH CONTROL INDICATOR
19A OIL QUANTITY INDICATOR (OR APC METER IF OIL
     QUANTITY INDICATOR IS NOT INSTALLED)
19B OIL WARNING INDICATOR

20 FUEL FLOW INDICATOR
21 EXHAUST NOZZLE POSITION INDICATOR
22 RAM AIR TURBINE EXTENSION HANDLE
23 EMERGENCY NOZZLE CLOSURE HANDLE
24 CLEARANCE PLANE AND ANTENNA TILT
     INDICATOR
25 CABIN ALTIMETER
26 EXTERNAL FUEL QUANTITY INDICATOR
27 INTERNAL FUEL QUANTITY INDICATOR
28 HYDRAULIC SYSTEM PRESSURE GAGES
29 RADAR MODE INDICATOR LIGHTS
30 RADAR INDICATOR
31 CANOPY JETTISON HANDLE
32 CONTROL TRANSFER PANEL
33 RUDDER PEDAL ADJUSTMENT HANDLE
34 ARMAMENT CONTROL PANEL
35 LANDING GEAR POSITION INDICATOR LIGHTS
36 DRAG CHUTE HANDLE
37 WING FLAP POSITION INDICATOR
38 MANUAL LANDING GEAR RELEASE HANDLE
39 FLAP ASYMMETRY WARNING LIGHT
     (1017 CW)

1 ANTENNA SELECT SWITCH
2 ANTI-G SUIT VALVE
3 STABILITY CONTROL SWITCHES
4 TRIM CONTROL PANEL
5 FUEL SHUTOFF SWITCH
6 RUDDER TRIM SWITCH
7 WING FLAP LEVER
8 THROTTLE
9 RADAR CONTROL PANEL
10 UHF COMMAND RADIO CONTROL PANEL
11 UHF EMERGENCY VOLUME CONTROL
12 CIRCUIT BREAKERS
13 MAP LIGHT

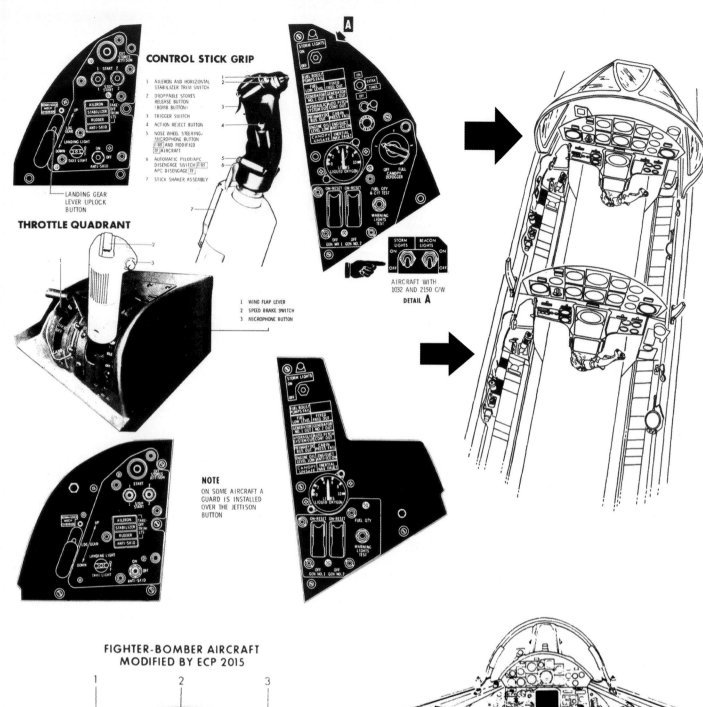

CONTROL STICK GRIP

1. AILERON AND HORIZONTAL STABILIZER TRIM SWITCH
2. DROPPABLE STORES RELEASE BUTTON (BOMB BUTTON)
3. TRIGGER SWITCH
4. ACTION REJECT BUTTON
5. NOSE WHEEL STEERING/MICROPHONE BUTTON (FIRE) AND MODIFIED (TF) AIRCRAFT
6. AUTOMATIC PILOT/APC DISENGAGE SWITCH (FIRE) APC DISENGAGE (TF)
7. STICK SHAKER ASSEMBLY

LANDING GEAR LEVER UPLOCK BUTTON

THROTTLE QUADRANT

1. WING FLAP LEVER
2. SPEED BRAKE SWITCH
3. MICROPHONE BUTTON

NOTE
ON SOME AIRCRAFT A GUARD IS INSTALLED OVER THE JETTISON BUTTON

AIRCRAFT WITH 1032 AND 2150 C/W
DETAIL **A**

FIGHTER-BOMBER AIRCRAFT MODIFIED BY ECP 2015

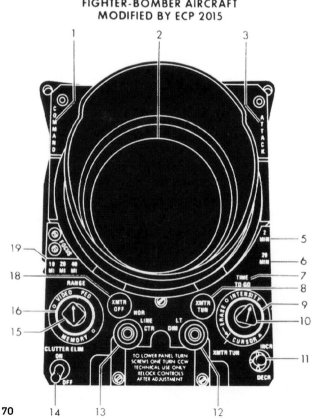

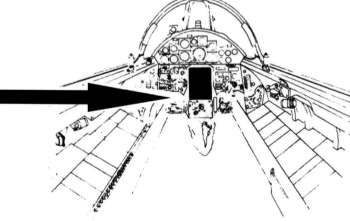

1 COMMAND LIGHT	11 TRANSMITTER TUNE SWITCH
2 RADAR SCREEN	12 LIGHT DIM DIAL
3 ATTACK LIGHT	13 HORIZON LINE CENTER DIAL
4 PUSH TO ERASE BUTTON	14 CLUTTER ELIMINATION SWITCH
5 TIME-TO-GO 2-MINUTE LIGHT	15 MEMORY DIAL
6 TIME-TO-GO 20-MINUTE LIGHT	16 VIDEO PEDESTAL DIAL
7 TIME-TO-GO LIGHT	17 RANGE LIGHTS (10 MI, 20 MI, 40 MI, 80 MI)
8 TRANSMITTER TUNE LIGHT	18 TRANSMITTER OFF-LIGHT
9 ERASE INTENSITY DIAL	19 RANGE LIGHTS (10 MI, 20 MI, 40 MI)
10 CURSOR DIAL	

Lockheed F-104C
Cockpit interior & instrument layout
(Photo: USAF)

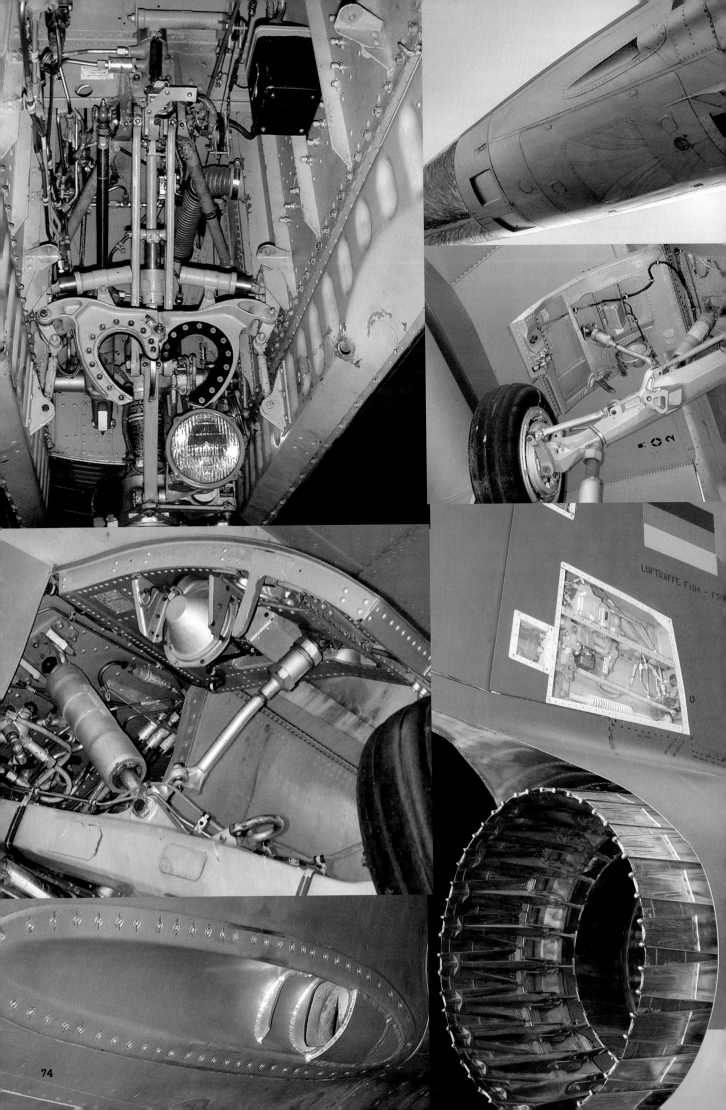

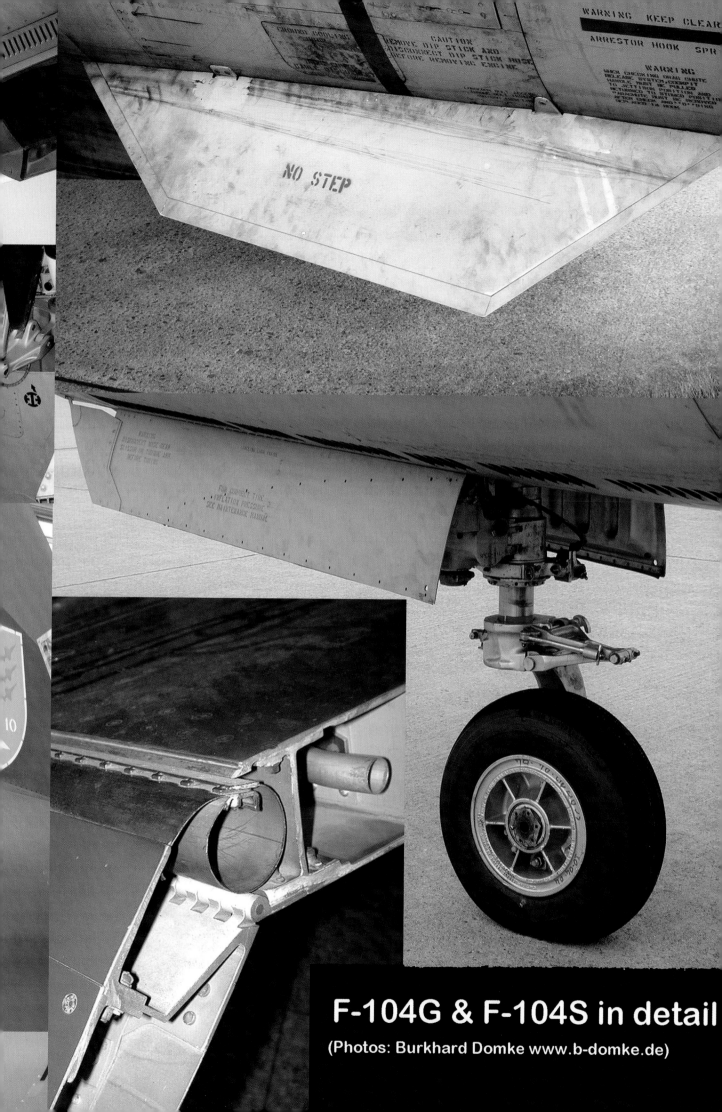

F-104G & F-104S in detail

(Photos: Burkhard Domke www.b-domke.de)

F-104G
Republic of China Air Force, 7th Squadron
3rd Tactical Fighter Wing
Unpainted finish with blue & white national insignia.

F-104G
Ejercito del Air, 104 Escuadron
Light grey finish with white wings
National insignia in yellow and red with unit markings on nose

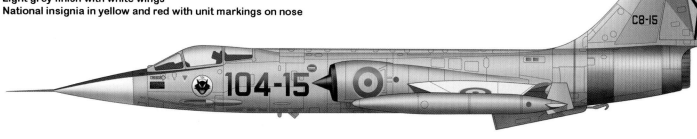

F-104G
Turkish Air Force, 191st Squadron
Unpainted finish with white wings.
National insignia in red and white.

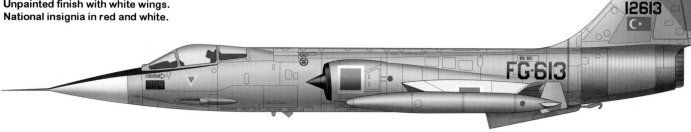

F-104J
Japanese Self Defense Force, 207 Squadron
Unpainted finish with white wings
Exercise markings in red and white
Unit emblem on tail in red, white and black.

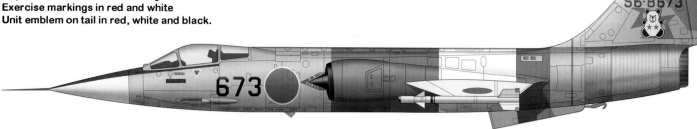

F-104N
National Aeronautics & Space Administration
Unpainted finish with white wings
Yellow and fluorescent orange trim outlined in black
Nasa emblem on intake

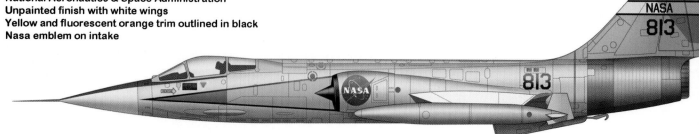

Illustrations by Ted Williams
www.tedwilliamsaviationart.co

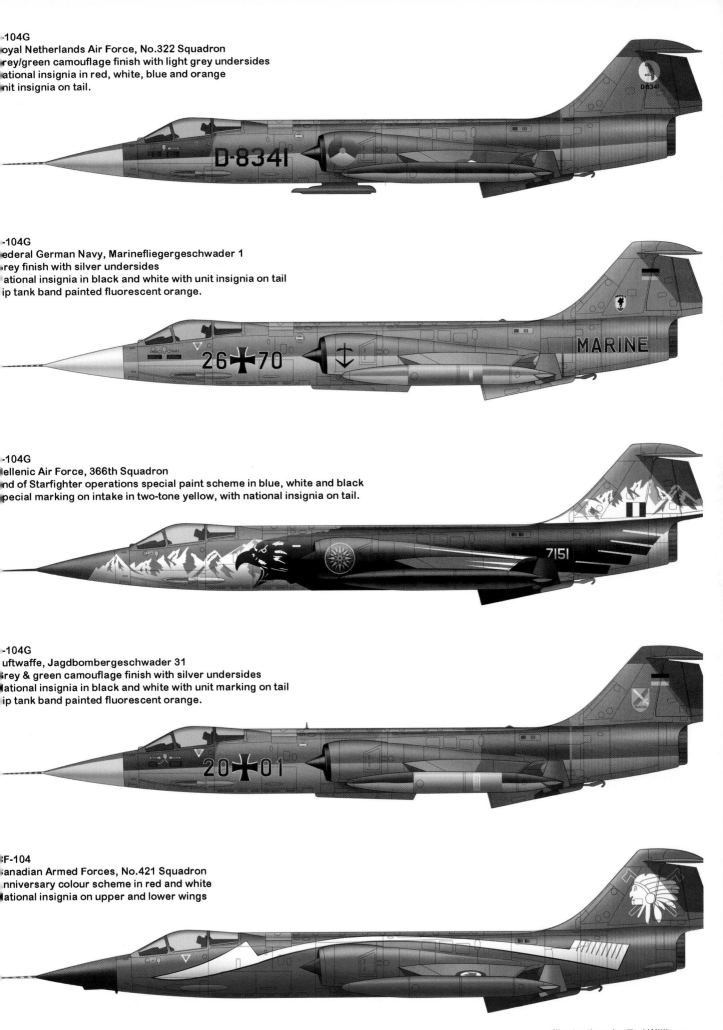

F-104G
Royal Netherlands Air Force, No.322 Squadron
Grey/green camouflage finish with light grey undersides
National insignia in red, white, blue and orange
Unit insignia on tail.

F-104G
Federal German Navy, Marinefliegergeschwader 1
Grey finish with silver undersides
National insignia in black and white with unit insignia on tail
Tip tank band painted fluorescent orange.

F-104G
Hellenic Air Force, 366th Squadron
End of Starfighter operations special paint scheme in blue, white and black
Special marking on intake in two-tone yellow, with national insignia on tail.

F-104G
Luftwaffe, Jagdbombergeschwader 31
Grey & green camouflage finish with silver undersides
National insignia in black and white with unit marking on tail
Tip tank band painted fluorescent orange.

CF-104
Canadian Armed Forces, No.421 Squadron
Anniversary colour scheme in red and white
National insignia on upper and lower wings

Illustrations by Ted Williams
www.tedwilliamsaviationart.com

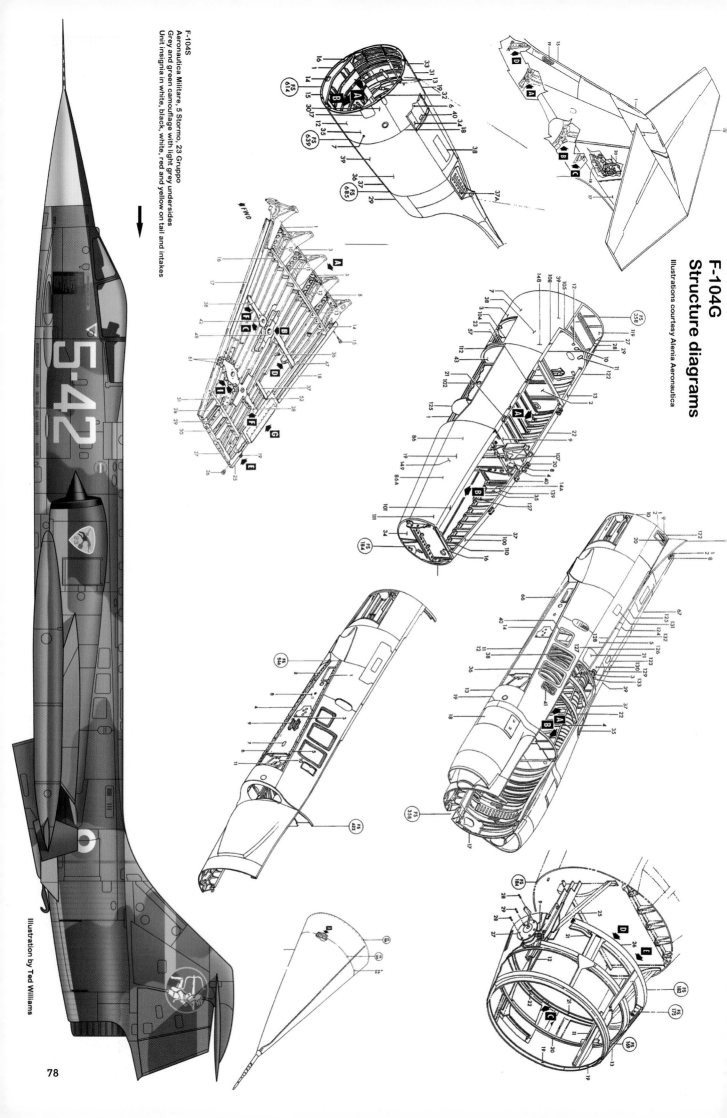

F-104G
Structure diagrams

Illustrations courtesy Alenia Aeronautica

F-104S
Aeronautica Militare, 5 Stormo, 23 Gruppo
Grey and green camouflage with light grey undersides
Unit insignia in white, black, white, red and yellow on tail and intakes

Illustration by Ted Williams

F-104G
Structure diagrams

Illustrations courtesy Alenia Aeronautica

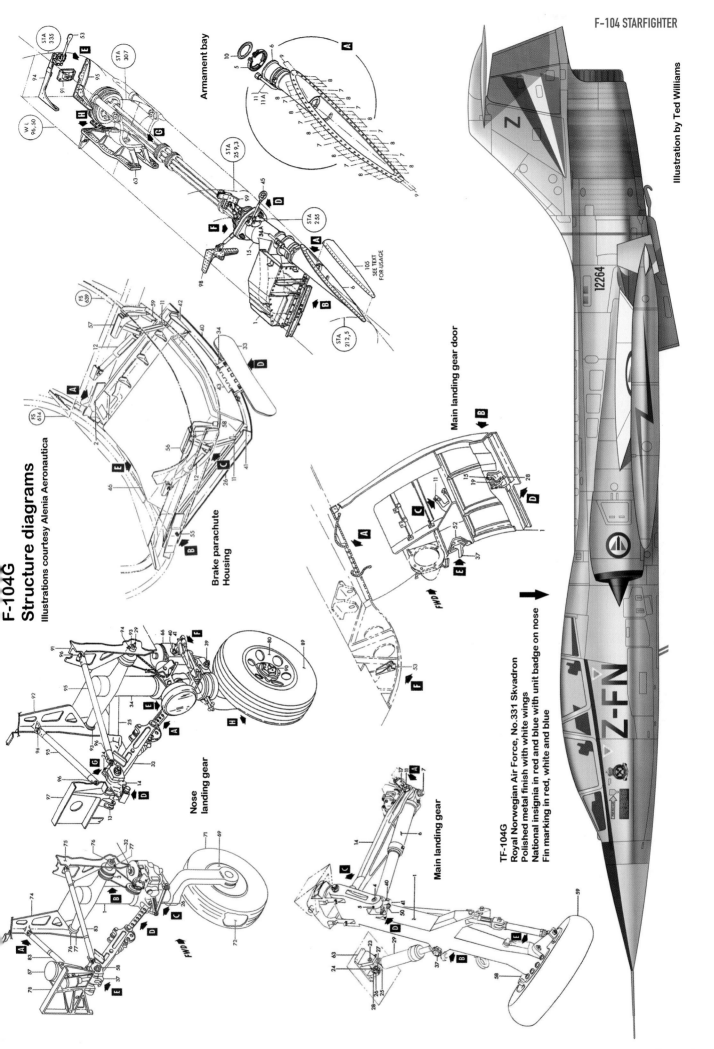

Illustration by Ted Williams

Armament bay

Brake parachute
Housing

Nose
landing gear

Main landing gear door

Main landing gear

TF-104G
Royal Norwegian Air Force, No.331 Skvadron
Polished metal finish with white wings
National insignia in red and blue with unit badge on nose
Fin marking in red, white and blue

12264

Z-FN

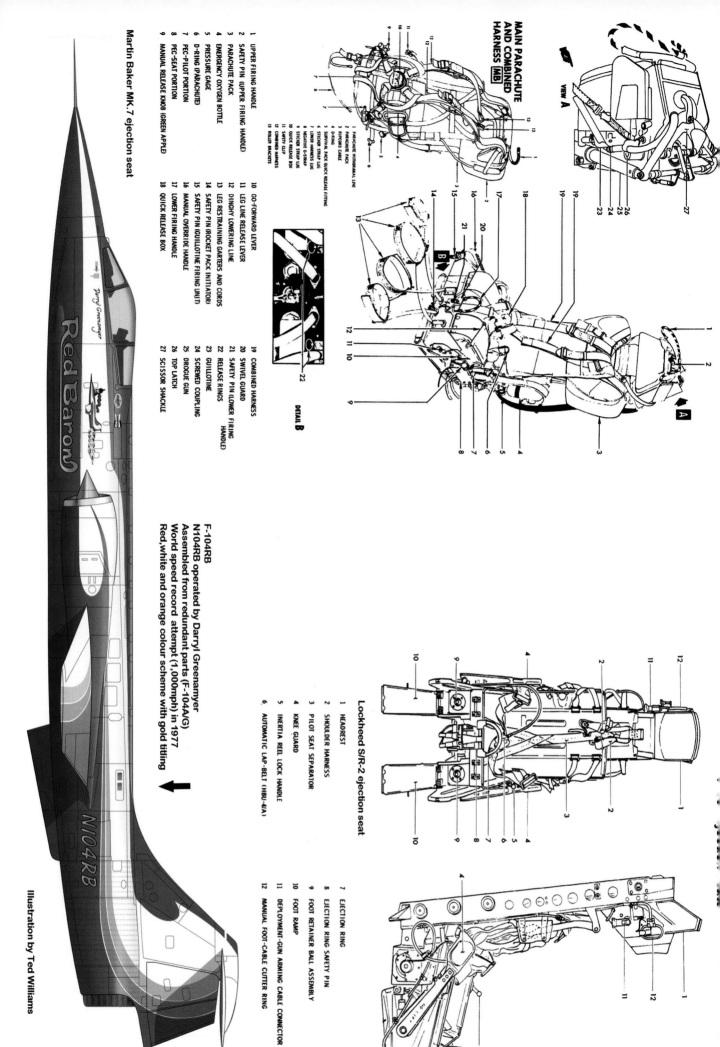

VIEW A

1 PARACHUTE WITHDRAWAL LINE
2 PARACHUTE PACK
3 RIPCORD CABLE
4 D-RING
5 SURVIVAL PACK QUICK RELEASE FITTING
6 STICKER STRAP LUG
7 LOWER HARNESS LUG
8 NEGATIVE G-STRAP
9 STICKER STRAP LUG
10 QUICK RELEASE BOX
11 SAFETY CLIP
12 COMBINED HARNESS
13 ROLLER BRACKETS

DETAIL B

Martin Baker Mk.7 ejection seat

1 UPPER FIRING HANDLE
2 SAFETY PIN (UPPER FIRING HANDLE)
3 PARACHUTE PACK
4 EMERGENCY OXYGEN BOTTLE
5 PRESSURE GAGE
6 D-RING (PARACHUTE)
7 PEC-PILOT PORTION
8 PEC-SEAT PORTION
9 MANUAL RELEASE KNOB (GREEN APPLE)
10 GO-FORWARD LEVER
11 LEG LINE RELEASE LEVER
12 DINGHY LOWERING LINE
13 LEG RESTRAINING GARTERS AND CORDS
14 SAFETY PIN (ROCKET PACK INITIATOR)
15 SAFETY PIN (GUILLOTINE FIRING UNIT)
16 MANUAL OVERRIDE HANDLE
17 LOWER FIRING HANDLE
18 QUICK RELEASE BOX
19 COMBINED HARNESS
20 SWIVEL GUARD
21 SAFETY PIN (LOWER FIRING HANDLE)
22 RELEASE RINGS
23 GUILLOTINE
24 SCREWED COUPLING
25 DROGUE GUN
26 TOP LATCH
27 SCISSOR SHACKLE

F-104RB
N104RB operated by Darryl Greenamyer
Assembled from redundant parts (F-104A/G)
World speed record attempt (1,000mph) in 1977
Red, white and orange colour scheme with gold titling

Illustration by Ted Williams

Lockheed S/R-2 ejection seat

1 HEADREST
2 SHOULDER HARNESS
3 PILOT SEAT SEPARATOR
4 KNEE GUARD
5 INERTIA REEL LOCK HANDLE
6 AUTOMATIC LAP-BELT (HBU-4/A)
7 EJECTION RING
8 EJECTION RING SAFETY PIN
9 FOOT RETAINER BALL ASSEMBLY
10 FOOT RAMP
11 DEPLOYMENT-GUN ARMING CABLE CONNECTOR
12 MANUAL FOOT-CABLE CUTTER RING

Lockheed NF-104

Illustration courtesy Lockheed Martin

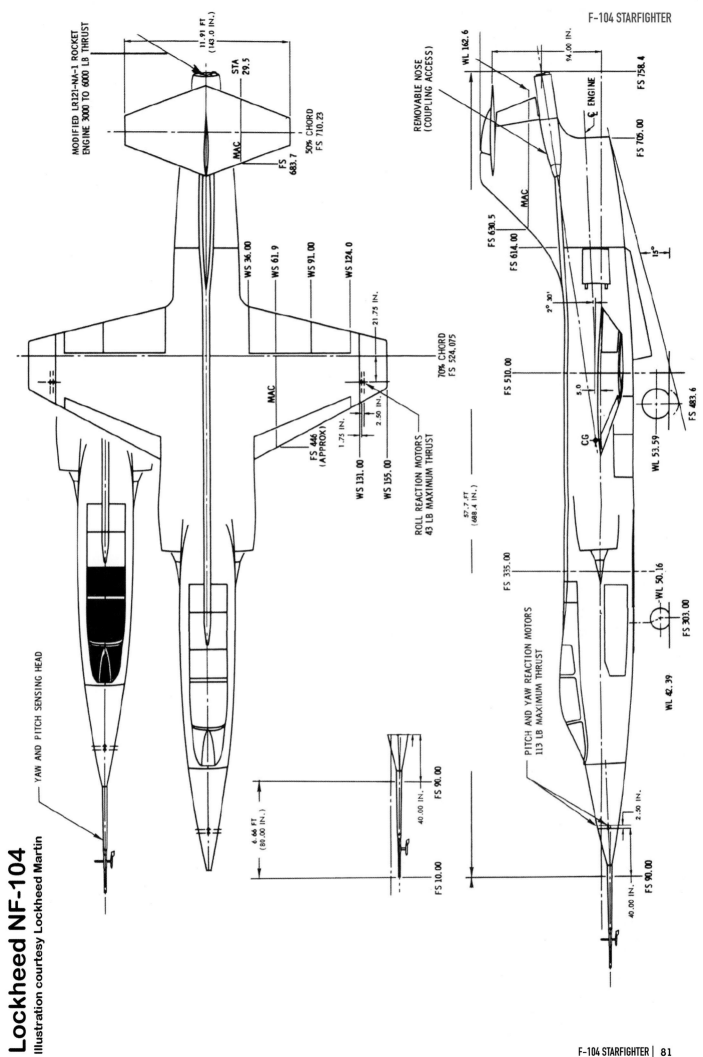

MODIFIED LR121-NA-1 ROCKET
ENGINE 3000 TO 6000 LB THRUST

11.91 FT
(143.0 IN.)

STA
29.5

50% CHORD
FS 710.23

MAC

FS
683.7

WS 36.00
WS 61.9
WS 91.00
WS 124.0

21.75 IN.

70% CHORD
FS 524.075

MAC

1.75 IN.
2.50 IN.

FS 446
(APPROX)

WS 131.00
WS 155.00

ROLL REACTION MOTORS
43 LB MAXIMUM THRUST

YAW AND PITCH SENSING HEAD

6.66 FT
(80.00 IN.)

40.00 IN.

FS 90.00

FS 10.00

WL 162.6

94.00 IN.

REMOVABLE NOSE
(COUPLING ACCESS)

FS 758.4

℄ ENGINE

FS 705.00

FS 630.5

MAC

FS 614.00

15°

2° 30'

FS 510.00

5.0

FS 483.6

CG

WL 53.59

FS 335.00

57.7 FT
(688.4 IN.)

WL 50.16

WL 42.39

FS 303.00

PITCH AND YAW REACTION MOTORS
113 LB MAXIMUM THRUST

2.50 IN.

FS 90.00

40.00 IN.

TWINS AND TEUTONICISM

Lockheed develops a dual-control trainer derivative of the Starfighter, and the F-104G joins the Luftwaffe's ranks

Desert ZELL. The F-104G roars skywards with rocket assistance during trials at Edwards AFB *(Photo: Lockheed)*

From the very start of the F-104 development process, Lockheed had proposed that a trainer variant of the Starfighter should be produced in parallel with the single seat interceptor. It was anticipated that both the USAF and any potential export customers would require a dual control version of the aircraft in which students could convert onto the type. The F-104B (company Model 283-93-03) emerged as a twin seat, dual-control trainer version of the F-104A model. A re-designed forward fuselage was created, with a second cockpit situated directly behind the original single cockpit position, under a new (longer) canopy layout. It was intended that the F-104B would have the same performance and combat capability of the F-104A although in order to provide space for the second seat, the 20-mm cannon of the F-104A was removed, and some internal electronic equipment was relocated. The internal fuel capacity had to be reduced from 897 to 752 US gallons, and the nose wheel assembly was reconfigured to retract rearwards. In all other respects the aircraft remained largely unchanged from the basic single seat design and the provision for two under-wing tanks plus two wing tip drop tanks was retained, thereby boosting total fuel capacity by some 730 US gallons. The

reduced armament capability was limited to a pair of wing tip-mounted AIM-9B Sidewinders, although the same AN/ASG-14T-1 fire control system was retained. The first of an initial batch of six F-104Bs (serial number 56-3719) took off on its maiden flight on 16 January 1967. This aircraft was in effect a "hand built" conversion from an existing F-104A airframe, and some features (such as the automatic pitch control system and the fire control system found in later aircraft) were not installed. It was unofficially designated as a YF-104B, and eventually it was brought up to production F-104B standard, used for sytems and flight testing, including trials associated with the downward-firing ejection seat that was initially fitted to the F-104A. Oddly, the initial batch of F-104Bs did not include the ventral fin that was fitted to the F-104A and during early testing, the F-104B exhibited directional stability problems, this snaking tendency being due to a lack of sufficient keel area. Twenty subsequent F-104B production versions (from FY 1957 batches) were therefore fitted with the F-104A's ventral fin and records fail to clarify why this necessary refinement was not incorporated from the outset. The aircraft also received a much larger vertical fin with broader chord and a fully power-assisted rudder, creating a fin

area that was 25 percent larger than that of the F-104A. The new trainer was initially powered by the J79-GE-3A, but this engine was later replaced by the more reliable J79-GE-3B as it became available, providing the aircraft with slightly more power and much greater reliability. Provision was also made for the withdrawal of the rear seat to facilitate the re-installation of the 20-mm rotary cannon, enabling the aircraft to operate as a single-seat combat aircraft if necessary, although this concept was not developed into a practical system and it was not used in any operational aircraft. The first USAF unit to receive the F-104B was the 83rd FIS at Hamilton AFB in California, where the first aircraft arrived early in 1958. Eventually, all three F-104A ADC squadrons received the F-104B with a nominal total of four aircraft being assigned to each squadron. Assigned primarily to conversion training, the aircraft could be used for combat training if necessary although without the cannon armament they were unsuitable for full combat operations, and although performance of the F-104B was almost identical to that of the F-104A, the lower internal fuel capacity reduced its effective range considerably. The F-104B was subject to many of the improvements that were made to the F-104A, including replacement

F-104B 56-3719 takes off on its maiden flight on 16 January 1967.
(Photo: USAF)

of the downward-firing ejection seats with C-2 upward-firing variants, although the cockpit canopy of the F-104B had not been designed to be blown off during the ejection sequence and the canopy had to be completely redesigned so that the new seat could be operated. The central section of the new tandem cockpit layout featured a clear separator that formed a windshield for the aft cockpit, should the forward canopy section be lost in flight or damaged. Air Defense Command's F-104Bs were transferred to the Air National Guard during 1960 and when the ANG squadrons operating the F-104A were called to active duty during the Berlin crisis of 1961 (deploying to Europe), some F-104B aircraft also joined the process. When the ANG squadrons reverted to state control in 1962, the F-104Bs were retained by the USAF

in the same way as the F-104As and returned to ADC for further service. The last of 26 F-104B aircraft was delivered in November of 1958, from an original total 106 that was ordered in 1957 and after many successful years of operations, the last F-104B left ADC service in 1969. Pakistan Air Force received two former USAF F-104Bs in 1960 together with the ten single-seat aircraft that were supplied to equip one squadron. At least two F-104Bs were also delivered to the Republic of China Air Force and in 1967 three F-104Bs were supplied to the Royal Jordanian Air Force. F-104B 53-1303 was transferred to NASA as Aircraft 819 in December 1959. The remainder of the small F-104B fleet was withdrawn to storage at Davis-Monthan AFB.

When the F-104C was put into production for TAC, a trainer derivative of this variant was

also required, and this resulted in the F-104D (Lockheed Model 383-04-06). The F-104D was largely similar to the F-104B, but it incorporated the improvements that had been made to the F-104C. From the outset it featured the large-area vertical fin design but like the F-104B it was not fitted with the 20-mm rotary cannon. The trainer's air-to-air armament was therefore limited to a pair of wingtip-mounted AIM-9B Sidewinders, although some aircraft were subsequently modified to enable two more Sidewinders to be carried under the forward fuselage. The F-104C's AN/ASG-14T-2 fire control system was fitted and the F-104C's provision for a removable in-flight refuelling probe of the F-104C was also included so that the aircraft's range could be increased if necessary, and students could also learn refueling

84

techniques in the trainer variant. Delivered with Lockheed C-1 downward-firing ejection seats, the later C-2 upward-firing seat was retrofitted, and the aircraft's canopy and windscreen arrangement was modified in line with the changes that were made to the F-104B. The F-104D earned the dubious distinction of becoming the last version of the Starfighter to be built for the USAF. Some 21 F-104Ds were delivered between November 1958 and August 1959, with all of the aircraft being assigned to the four squadrons of the 479th Tactical Fighter Wing that had already been equipped with F-104Cs. A further 83 F-104Ds ordered under FY 1957 funding were subsequently cancelled when the USAF prematurely ended all of its Starfighter procurement plans. As with the F-104C, some F-104Ds were

eventually transferred to the Puerto Rico Air National Guard in 1967 where they remained in use until July 1975. However most of the F-104D aircraft went into storage at Davis-Monthan AFB, other than six aircraft that were supplied to Taiwan.

Following the development of the F-104G "Super Starfighter" for Germany (and eventually other Nato countries) Lockheed proceeded with a linear programme to create a dual-control variant of the aircraft. The TF-104G (Lockheed Model 583-10-20) was a combat-capable development of the F-104G, following the same conversion process that had been applied to the F-104B and F-104D. It featured a cockpit canopy similar to that of the F-104D, with a fixed transparent area separating the two separate canopy hoods. Fitted with the NASARR fire control system of

the single-seat F-104G, it was also equipped with under-wing pylon positions that could carry the same offensive weapons that the single-seat F-104G was cleared to release. However, unlike the F-104G, the TF-104G did not include the centerline weapons point, and the 20-mm Vulcan cannon was deleted, with internal equipment relocated and fuel capacity reduced. Lockheed was responsible for the manufacture of every TF-104G produced, although some aircraft incorporated components that were supplied by the European Starfighter consortium that was set-up as part of the huge export programme. Because the TF-104G aircraft was a direct development of the F-104G and was subject to the same design changes that had been applied to the F-104D, there was no requirement for a prototype airframe, and

The first dual-control Starfighter was F-104B 56-3719. As can be seen, the two-piece canopy arrangement does not feature the central (fixed) clear section that was common to subsequent Starfighter trainer derivatives.
(Photo: USAF)

F-104B prototype 56-3719 pictured next to Lockheed's T2V Seastar, which was probably being used during 1957 as a chase aircraft for the Starfighter. *(Photo: Lockheed)*

Aviatrix Jacqueline Cochran was the first female pilot to break the sound barrier, although she is credited with a number of significant aerospace records, including a Federation Aeronautique Internationale speed record of 1,203.94mph over a 100km circuit, and 1,273.2mph over a 25km course, set in 1963, using TF-104G N104L. She is pictured in Lockheed TF-104G, 56-3719, with Chuck Yeager in 1961. *(Photo: Lockheed)*

F-104D 57-1333, operated by the USAF's Tactical Air Command until 1973, when it was placed into storage at AMARC (Davis-Monthan AFB). It languished here until 1982 and is now on permanent external display at that California Science Center, Los Angeles. *(Photo: USAF)*

the first aircraft to be completed was a production model. Lockheed built a total of 220 TF-104Gs (including 48 aircraft assembled from components supplied by the European Starfighter consortium) in six versions, identified by adding a suffix applied to their Model 583 company designations. Models 583C to 583H were versions manufactured for MAP delivery to Germany and Italy, or direct delivery to Holland, Germany, Belgium, and Italy. Before production of the F-104G could get underway, the Luftwaffe was already keen to begin the long transition onto the F-104, and there was an obvious need for two-seat trainer Starfighters that could be used to train Luftwaffe instructors. This urgency resulted in the F-104F (company Model 483-04-08), a minimum- change derivative of

the F-104D combat trainer. Powered by the J79-GE-11A turbojet, it lacked the all-weather NASARR fire-control system of the F-104G and was not designed to be combat-capable. Whilst it didn't have the F-104G's "beefed up" airframe, it was fitted with a Martin-Baker ejection seat. Some 30 examples were built for the Luftwaffe, the first being handed over at Palmdale in October 1959. Initially, they were based in the United States and carried standard USAF markings plus USAF serial numbers (59-4994 to 59-5023). After being used to train the initial cadre of German instructors they were transferred to the Luftwaffe's Waffenschule 10 based at Norvenich in Germany, with Luftwaffe serial numbers (BB360 to BB389) (during January 1968 these serial numbers were changed to 2901 to 2930.) The F-104F Starfighter trainers

were withdrawn from Luftwaffe service in December 1971 when the TF-104G assumed the training role. Mention should also be made of one famous aircraft from the Model 583D fleet that was retained by Lockheed as a demonstration aircraft. With civil registration number N104L it was nicknamed "Free World Defender" and suitably decorated as such. Used for demonstration flying, it was also flown by the famous aviatrix Jacqueline Cochran to set three women's world speed records. On 11 May 1964, she flew an average speed of 1429.3 mph over a 15/25 km course, and on 1 June she flew at an average speed of 1303.18 mph over a 100-km closed-circuit course. Two days later she flew at an average speed of 1127.4 mph over a 500-km closed-circuit course. This well-known aircraft was eventually delivered to the Koninklijke

Delivered on 10 April 1959 to the 479th Tactical Fighter Wing. F-104D 67-1234 was transferred to the Systems Command at Eglin AFB in June 1967. It then moved to the Armament Development & Test Center and finally the 198th TFS of 156th Tactical Fighter Group (Puerto Rico Air National Guard), in June 1972. On 20December 1972 it crashed following an air refueling exercise accident. *(Photo: USAF)*

F-104F 59-4997 was given the Luftwaffe code BB+363 and was used for training the first German pilots at Palmdale during February 1960. It was shipped to Germany in June 1960 and joined WaSLw 10 (the Luftwaffe's Operational Training Unit) in October 1960. It was withdrawn in April 1971 and stored at Erding AB before being scrapped at Fassberg during the mid-1980s. *(Photo: Lockheed)*

F-104F 59-4999 was shipped to Bremerhaven in Germany during June 1960. It was assigned to WaSLw on 26 July 1960. The aircraft crashed on 19 June 1962 during practice for an air show formation display following lead pilot disorientation in clouds on June 19, 1962. *(Photo: Lockheed)*

Luchtmacht (KLu) with the Dutch Air Force serial number D-5072.

West German's Luftwaffe eventually received a total of 915 Starfighters, comprising 30 F-104Fs, 96 F-104Gs, and 136 TF-104Gs from Lockheed, 255 F/RF-104Gs from the North Group, 210 F-104Gs from the South Group, 88 F-104Gs from the West Group, 50 F/RF-104Gs from the Italian Group, plus 50 replacement F-104Gs from MBB to replace some of those lost in crashes).

At their peak in the mid-1970s, Starfighters equipped five nuclear-armed Luftwaffe fighter-bomber wings, two interceptor wings, and two reconnaissance wings. In addition, two attack wings of the Marineflieger (Federal German Navy) were equipped with Starfighters. The first German Starfighters to enter service were the Lockheed-built two-seat F-104Fs which were initially used in the USA to train German instructors. At that time, the F-104Fs were painted with standard USAF insignia and carried USAF serial numbers. These machines were then handed over to Waffenschule 10, which was based at Norvenich in Germany. After handover, they were repainted in Luftwaffe insignia and assigned German serial numbers, and conversion of pilots for JBG31 began in July of 1960.

The first operational unit to be equipped with the F-104G was Jagdbombergeschwader 31 "Boelcke, also based at Norvenich, and becoming fully operational in 1963. More units swiftly followed, beginning with JBG32 at Lechfeld, and then JBG33 at Buchel, JBG34 at Memmingen, and JBG36 at Rheine-Hopsten. Two fighter wings also received the F-104G, these being JG71 at Wittmundhafen and JG74 at Neuburg. Additionally, two Aufklarungsgeschwadern (reconnaissance wings) were equipped with the reconnaissance-configured RF-104G, these being AKG51 at Ingoldstadt and AKG52 at Leck. The Federal German Navy also re-equipped with Starfighters and both MFG1 at Schleswig and MFG2 at Eggebeck received a mix of F-104G and RF-104G aircraft (plus trainers) for their armed reconnaissance and anti-shipping strike roles. Germany's huge re-equipment programme required an equally ambitious training system that would enable Germany to produce capable pilots in substantial numbers. Northern European weather and stifling operational restrictions placed severe limitations on the amount of useful training that could be done in Germany, and following discussions between the US Government, Lockheed and the USAF, Germany set up a Luftwaffe training operation in the United States, where there was unlimited space, and weather conditions that were perfect for intensive flying training. Luftwaffe Starfighters were withdrawn from the delivery process and diverted directly to Luke AFB in Arizona where they were assigned to the 4512th, 4518th, and 4443rd Combat Crew Training Squadrons of the USAF. Although remaining under the ownership of Germany's Luftwaffe, these aircraft carried USAF insignia and were assigned USAF serial numbers. All of the Luftwaffe's initial training on the Starfighter was concentrated at Luke AFB, while advanced training for the European environment (including weapons training), was performed by Waffenschule 10 based at Jever. As the Starfighter settled into service with the Luftwaffe, the aircraft's accident rate soon began to increase, following the first two losses in 1961 when intensive flight

TF-104G 61-3074 made its first flight in 1963, joining the Luftwaffe and the 4510 CCTW at Luke AFB. It remained here until July 1983 when it was sold to the USAF before being transferred to Taiwan under project "Ali Shan No.8". It was withdrawn in the late 1980s and moved to Ching Chuan Kang as an airfield decoy. *(Photo: USAF)*

operations began. A further seven crashes occurred in 1962, and by 1965 the annual loss rate had risen to 28, or an average of more than two every month. By 1966 no less than 60 German Starfighters had crashed, with a loss of 35 pilots. This disturbing accident rate eventually peaked at an equivalent of 139 losses per 100,000 flying hours. It was hardly surprising that Germany's newspapers were alerted to the issue and the story slowly grew into a national scandal, resulting in the appearance of many derogatory nicknames for the F-104 that were almost impossible to shake off. The Starfighter became better

known as the "Widowmaker" and "Flying Coffin" instead of being regarded as a vital national asset. It was even suggested by some (presumably with tongue firmly in cheek) that if one was prepared to wait long enough, almost every square mile of Germany would eventually have a Starfighter crash into it. The media asserted (often without foundation) that there were serious problems with the Starfighter's performance and reliability, and that in simple terms the aircraft was unsafe to fly. In reality, the Starfighter didn't suffer from any deficiencies at all, and it was the Luftwaffe's inability to

TF-104G 63-8454 joined the 4510th CCTW at Luke AFB 1in 1963 and remained here for 20 years before being sold to the USAF pending delivery to Taiwan in 1984 under project "Ali Shan No.8". It was assigned to No.3 Wing at Ching Chuan Kang AB. It was withdrawn from use in April 1993 and is now on display in the Veterans Military Cemetery in Kaohsiung City.

TF-104G (construction number 583D-5702, model 583-10-20) was retained by Lockheed as a demonstrator aircraft, carrying the civil registration number N104L/N90500 and named "Free World Defender." Jacqueline Cochran set two women's world speed records in this aircraft. Lockheed then refurbished the aircraft before transferring it to the Koninklijke Luchtmacht (KLU) with the RNLAF serial D-5702. When the RNLAF withdrew its Starfighter fleet the aircraft was sent to Turkey during August 1980 with new serial number 5702. *(Photos: Lockheed)*

safely operate the aeroplane that was at the root cause of the growing problem. The media stories eventually brought the issue to the Bonn Government, where politicians claimed that the entire Starfighter programme had been a political misjudgment.

The press left many people with the impression that there was something intrinsically wrong with the F-104G, that it was just too difficult an airplane to fly for the new and relatively inexperienced Luftwaffe pilots. The high loss rate generated a flurry of criticism of the Bonn government, some

critics claiming that the entire Starfighter program had been politically-motivated and should be cancelled outright. Over the Starfighter's complete period of service in Germany, approximately 270 losses occurred, representing almost 30 percent of the total number of aircraft purchased. However, this figure wasn't proportionally higher than those that were attained by other countries, and in Canada the Royal Canadian Air Force ultimately lost more than half of it's CF-104G fleet in flying accidents. It is therefore odd to note how Germany's losses were (and still are) often regarded as unusually high,

especially when an even higher 36 percent attrition rate applied to the F-104G's predecessor, the Republic F-84F Thunderstreak. However, in direct comparison, the Royal Norwegian Air Force accrued 56,000 flying hours on Starfighters for the loss of only six airframes, while the Spanish Air Force managed to operate the Starfighter from delivery to withdrawal without the loss of so much as a single example. Some of the Luftwaffe losses could certainly be traced to technical problems with the F-104G aircraft rather that deficiencies in pilot ability. Engine

F-104G KF+134 was assigned to the 6516th Flight Line Maintenance Squadron at Edwards AFB with the US/German Joint Test Force team in 1962 for early test flights. It was airlifted to Messerschmitt at Manching in July,1962 and joined JaboG 31 in September 1962 in Silver-finish colors, recoded as DA+106 in December. It was destroyed on 30 July 1969 at Norvenich AB when an inaccurate speed indication (caused by a heavy nose wheel shimmy) led to an aborted take off. The aircraft ran off the runway and caught fire, its pilot ejecting to safety. *(Photo: Lockheed)*

RF-104G KG+322 made its first flight on 16 March 1964, joining Aufklärungsgeschwader 51 in June 1966. It was airlifted to the USA a few weeks later for Sideways Looking Radar trials with Lockheed at Palmdale. It was fitted with a modified nose section and equipped with an external reconnaissance pod, re-designated as an RF-104G-1. Although the tests were successful, the SLAR programme was abandoned when the Luftwaffe opted to purchase the RF-4E. The aircraft was airlifted to MBB in March 1972 but conversion to standard RF-104G standard did not proceed and the aircraft was withdrawn from use. It is now on display at Erding AB. *(Photos: Lockheed)*

This magnificent line-up of F-104G Starfighters is led by JD+107, which was manufactured by SABCA in Belgium, making its first flight on 20 December 1963. It was delivered to JG 74 during June 1964 and remained in Luftwaffe service until 7 November 1974 when it was withdrawn with with 1.601 flight hours to its credit. It was scrapped at Erding AB in December 1978. (Photo: Tim McLelland collection)

The Luftwaffe's concerns over airfield vulnerability led to the ZELL (ZEro Length Launch) project, which explored the possibility of launching Starfighters (armed with atomic bombs) from mobile ramps, using a Rocketdyne motor to launch the aircraft to take off climbing speed. At this stage the rocket booster would fall away and the aircraft would continue on its mission, recovering to temporary landing strips that would probably have been created on stretches of autobahnen. Trials were conducted at Edwards AFB, followed by further trials at Lechfeld, where two trials aircraft were flown by both Lockheed and JGB 32 pilots. The trials were successful but the project was eventually abandoned. *(Photos: Lockheed)*

malfunctions included problems with the J79's variable afterburner nozzle, and contamination of the Starfighter's liquid oxygen system caused pilot loss of consciousness in some accidents that were investigated. The automatic pitch-up limiter was prone to failure during high-speed and low-altitude flying or in tight turns, and this resulted in its temporary removal, resulting in restrictions on the aircraft's manoeuvrability. The Starfighter required between 38 and 45 hours of maintenance for every hour in the air, and many of the Luftwaffe's ground crew personnel were conscripts who were probably either too hastily trained, or insufficiently educated in the requirements of what was a relatively complex machine when compared to its predecessor. But the main contributory factor in many accidents was pilot error, and there were obvious reasons why this was occurring. The most obvious was the relatively low number of flying hours allocated to pilot training (some 13-15 hours per month as compared to a Nato average of around 20), but another very significant factor was that most pilot training was completed in the USA, where USAF procedures applied and where training was conducted in perfect weather conditions. The situation in Germany was very different, and stringent operational procedures applied in the regions where Luftwaffe Starfighters operated, often in extremely poor weather conditions at low level. Consequently, the

Luftwaffe pilots had a much higher cockpit workload and when this was combined with relatively little experience and a demanding aircraft that required constant attention, it was inevitable that catastrophes would occur.

When Germany's Starfighter crisis reached its peak in 1966, Luftwaffe chief General Wernher Panitzki was forced to resign after claiming that the Starfighter procurement project had been politically driven. His successor was World War Two ace Lieutenant General Johannes Steinhoff, who had flown Me.262 jet fighters during the war. Steinhoff had not been a supporter of the Starfighter programme, and he had already made recommendations on F-104G survival measures to the German Defence Ministry, but his proposals had been ignored. Once he assumed his new position he immediately began to look at ways in which pilot survivability could be improved, starting with the aircraft's escape system. The Lockheed C-2 ejection seat that had initially been installed in the F-104G had been fitted with a

more powerful Talley Corporation rocket booster during 1966 to give it a true zero-zero capability. However, the Talley rockets had a destabilizing effect on the seat after ejection, and they had to be removed and when further modifications were made to the C-2 seats in December 1966, it was agreed that the Lockheed seat should be abandoned in favour of the more reliable Martin-Baker Mk GQ7A zero-zero ejection seat. A contract was signed on 8 March 1967 to re-equip the entire German F-104G fleet with the Martin-Baker seat and this process was completed over a period of twelve months. The seat was put to test for the first time on 24 September 1968 when a pilot successfully ejected following an aborted overshoot at Ramstein AFB. In order to to reduce the Starfighter accident rate (rather than improving the means of escaping from what seemed to have almost become inevitable crashes), a thorough revision was made of the Luftwaffe's training techniques and procedures and by 1968 the serious accident rate had almost halved, although the numbers began to rise slightly and eventually settled at around 10-12 per year. This was still rather more than many would have liked, but it was regarded as a more acceptable figure, given the numbers of active aircraft, the huge combined numbers of

hours being flown, and the very demanding environment in which they operated. Primarily, the Luftwaffe's Starfighters were assigned to the tactical strike role, carrying a single B-43 nuclear store under the fuselage on the centerline pylon, and up to 250 Luftwaffe Starfighters were committed to NATO's nuclear force. At the height of the Cold War, each of the fighter-bomber wings maintained a force of six nuclear-armed Starfighters on 24-hour Quick Reaction Alert, prepared to scramble within 17 minutes of an order being issued. The weapons were held under American control however, and could not be released to the Luftwaffe units without direct orders from the USAF, through a chain of command from the President. For other

non-nuclear attack profiles, a typical load of conventional weapons for ground attack included Lepus flare bombs, CBU-33 cluster bombs, a variety of free-fall HE bombs and LAU-3A unguided rocket packs. Outside of the Luftwaffe's sphere of operations, a fleet of 15◄ aircraft was also allocated to the Federal Germ Navy, divided between two naval attack wing Primarily dedicated to the maritime environment, the aircraft were normally arme with MBB Kormoran anti-ship missiles, with o weapon attached to each main wing pylon. With a range of up to 23 miles, the missile had 350lb warhead with 16 radially mounted projectile charges and fuse delays, designed f penetration of armoured structure. After laun

F-104G Starfighters were first assigned to MFG2 during 1960, replacing a fleet of aged Seahawks. They remained in use until 1986 when the type was retired, following the arrival of Tornado. *(Photos: Axel Ostermann)*

the missile employed an inertial mid-course guidance system in conjunction with a radio altimeter to maintain an altitude of less than 100 feet above sea level during the final approach to the target. The radar seeker in the nose could operate either as an active radar seeker or as a passive receiver, and when it locked onto its target, the impact point was calculated to be just above the waterline of the vessel in order to ensure maximum damage. The Naval Starfighters also employed other weapons if necessary, including bombs and rocket projectiles and like the Luftwaffe, they also maintained a fleet or RF-104G aircraft, equipped with camera systems (usually the KS-67A) located

in the forward fuselage (replacing the cannon armament). The camera system resulted in the appearance of a bulged fairing under the forward fuselage that resulted in small modifications to the nose landing gear doors. Some Luftwaffe and Navy aircraft were eventually reconfigured as standard F-104G aircraft and a few F-104Gs were modified to reconnaissance standard. The controversial introduction of the Starfighter in Germany tarred the aircraft with a reputation that it didn't deserve, but despite this, the F-104 is still often regarded as an unusually dangerous machine even to the present day. In fact, it was no more troublesome than any of its

contemporaries, and it was a combination of inadequate training, poor maintenance techniques, and a risky operational environment that conspired to create so many accidents – and of course the sheer numbers of aircraft that were being operated. Ironically, by the time that Germany finally relinquished its Starfighters, the aircraft was regarded as a magnificent warplane that had performed very well. It was reliable and fast, and tough enough for the low level environment in which it was often forced to operate. Despite its reputation as the "Widowmaker" the Starfighter proved itself to be a remarkably versatile and effective fighting machine. ❖

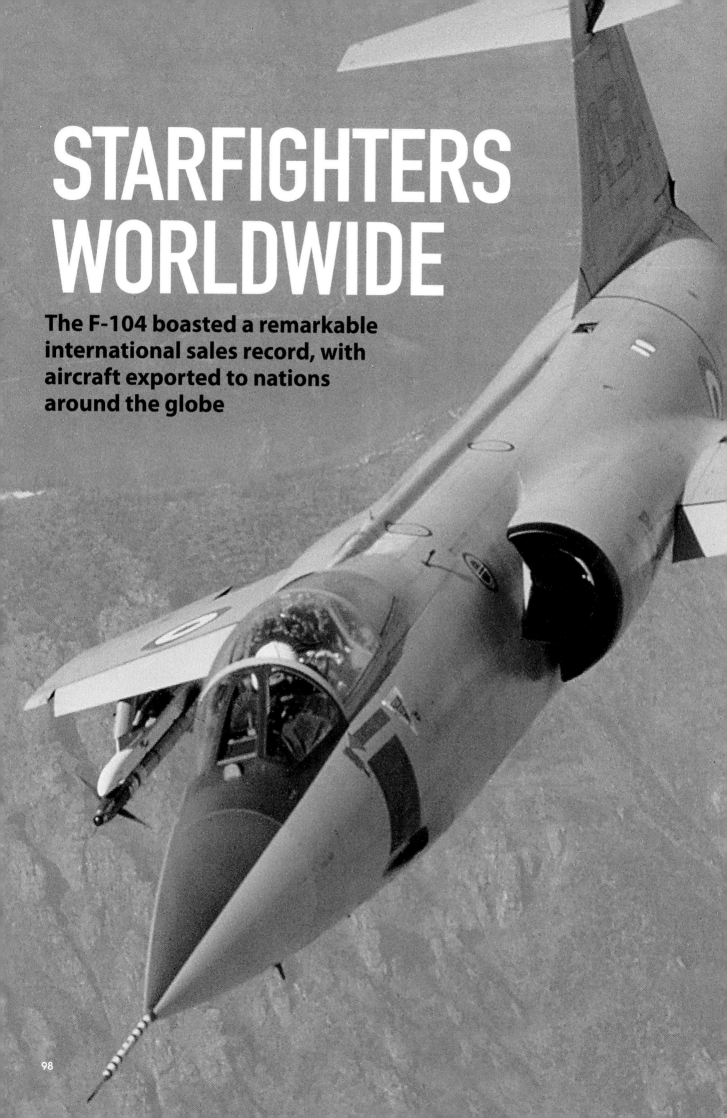

STARFIGHTERS WORLDWIDE

The F-104 boasted a remarkable international sales record, with aircraft exported to nations around the globe

Belgium

When Nato countries opted to purchase the Starfighter, it was almost inevitable that Belgium would do likewise. Some 112 Starfighters were purchased for the Belgian Air Force, the order divided between 100 F-104G aircraft (serial FX-01 to FX-100), and 12 TF-104G trainers (serial FC-01 to FC-12). Only 40 of the F-104Gs were MDAP-funded, with the remainder being directly financed by the Belgian government. The first of the F-104G airframes arrived from the USA by sea, in disassembled form, although almost all Belgian aircraft were manufactured and assembled at the SABCA Gosselies plant, together with 88 F-104Gs that were destined for Germany's Luftwaffe. The first three trainer aircraft for Belgium were TF-104F variants, manufactured at Lockheed's Palmdale plant, with the remaining nine TF-104Gs being assembled by SABCA from Lockheed CKD ("Complete Knock Down") kits, although the three TF-104Fs were eventually updated to TF-104G standard. Destined to replace Avro Canada CF-100 Mk.5 Canucks and Republic F-84F Thunderstreaks, No.1 Wing received its first Starfighters in April 1963, followed by No.10 Wing from June 1964. Aircraft were rotated between the two wings (and the

Belgium acquired 101 Starfighters, the single seat F-104Gs being manufactured indigenously by SABCA, while the TF-104G trainers were built by Lockheed. One F-104G crashed before delivery. *(Photo: Tim McLelland collection)*

component squadrons) in order to maintain fatigue life, and some aircraft were retained in storage as attrition replacements. While No.1 Wing was assigned to air defence, No.10 Wing assumed the strike-attack role, with Starfighters placed on 24-hour alert status, armed with American B-61 free-fall nuclear bombs (from 1972 onwards, smaller tactical nuclear bombs were brought into service). Belgium's Starfighter phase-out began late in 1979 and ended October 1983, when all of the remaining active aircraft were withdrawn and either placed in storage at Koksijde, or transferred (in the case of MDAP airframes) to the Turkish Air Force.

Belgian Air Force

1 Wing, BAF based at Beauvechain
349th Squadron
350th Squadron
10 Wing, BAF based at Kleine Brogel
23rd Squadron
31st Squadron

Netherlands

A total of 138 Starfighters joined the Koninklijke Luchtmacht (Royal Netherlands Air Force), comprising 95 F/RF-104Gs

manufactured by the North group (Fokker), 25 F-104Gs manufactured by Fiat's Italian group, and 18 TF-104Gs manufactured by Lockheed. Entering service during December 1962 (assigned to No. 306 Squadron based at Twenthe), the Starfighters were destined to replace Republic F-84F/RF-84Fs that had been in service for many years. No.306 Squadron was the Operational Conversion Unit for the Starfighter until January 1964, when a Training and Conversion Unit was established at Leeuwarden. The F-104G was assigned to the interceptor with Nos.322 and 323 Squadrons based at Leeuwarden, and assigned to the fighter-bomber role with Nos.311 and 312 Squadrons based at Volkel. After many years of satisfactory service, conversion onto the F-16 began in 1979, and the last operational Starfighters were withdrawn from use late in November 1984. Some 43 Starfighters (35.8 percent of the force) were ultimately lost in flying accidents, although this figure was not deemed to be unreasonably high, given the type's extensive use in a demanding environment. Most of the withdrawn Starfighters were eventually transferred to Greece and Turkey for further service.

The Belgian Air Force operated the Starfighter from February 1963 until September 1983. Redundant aircraft were sent to Turkey and Taiwan. *(Photo: Tim McLelland collection)*

Seen during the mid-1960s, this BAF TF-104 illustrates the open braking parachute bay under the lower fuselage. Delivered unpainted with white wings, Belgium's aircraft were eventually camouflaged in a two-tone green and brown paint scheme similar to the USAF's contemporary finish. *(Photo: Tim McLelland collection)*

The Koninklijke Luchtmacht (Royal Netherlands Air Force) operated a fleet of 138 Starfighters, some of which were RF–104G aircraft allocated to the reconnaissance role. As can be seen, this variant featured a bulged fairing under the forward fuselage, behind which the camera sensors were housed. The fairing extended onto the landing gear doors. The light grey paint finish was soon replaced by grey and green camouflage. *(Photo: Tim McLelland collection)*

Later in the Starfighter's service with the RNLAF, a number of F-104G aircraft were re-assigned to reconnaissance operations, equipped with an Orpheus reconnaissance pod that could be carried under the fuselage. *(Photo: Tim McLelland)*

Denmark obtained 25 F-104G aircraft together with four TF-104G trainers as part of a Mutual Defense Assistance Act arrangement during 1964-5. Additional aircraft were obtained in 1971-3 when 15 CF-104 and seven F-104D aircraft were supplied by Canadair. *(Photo: RDAF)*

Royal Netherlands Air Force

306 Squadron RNLAF
311 Squadron RNLAF
312 Squadron RNLAF
322 Squadron RNLAF
323 Squadron RNLAF
Training and Conversion Unit A
Conversie Afdeling Volkel

Denmark

The Kongelige Danske Flyvevaben (Royal Danish Air Force) received twenty-five Canadian-built F-104Gs and four Lockheed-built TF-104Gs from the US Mutual Aid Program during November 1964. These were assigned to two units; Esk 723 and Esk 726, both based at Aalborg, with the first aircraft being officially accepted into service on 29 June 1965. Expansion of the RDAF Starfighter

fleet took place from 1972 when 22 former Canadian Forces aircraft (15 CF-104s and seven CF-104D trainers) were acquired. Some were used as attrition replacements, although the CF-104Ds were modified for the electronic counter measures role before delivery to Esk 726. Withdrawal of the Starfighter fleet began in 1983 with Esk 723 disbanding on 1 January. Esk 726 remained active until 30 April 1986, after which all of the RDAF Starfighters were withdrawn, apart from four aircraft that survived in the target facilities role for some time. Over the 21 years of active service, only 12 Starfighters were lost in accidents (a rate of 23.5 percent) and following the introduction of the F-16 into service, many former RADF Starfighters were transferred to Taiwan in 1987 for further use.

Royal Danish Air Force

Eskadrille 723 based, Aalborg Air Base
Eskadrille 726 based, Aalborg Air Base

Italy

The Aeronautica Militare Italiana (AMI) received 125 Fiat-built F-104Gs (including 11 RF-104Gs) plus 12 Lockheed-manufactured TF-104Gs and 16 Fiat-manufactured TF-104Gs. The Starfighter entered service in 1963, equipping three interceptor squadrons, one fighter-bomber squadron, two reconnaissance squadrons and a training unit. A further seven Lockheed TF-104Gs were transferred from the Luftwaffe in 1984 although not all of these entered service (some being used as spares sources). Italy's 1965 AWX (All-Weather Interceptor) design competition led to an

▲ Denmark's Starfighters regularly flew with Sidewinder missile rails (and missiles) attached to the forward fuselage. During the late 1960s the RDAF Starfighter fleet received a green camouflage finish. The green paint was affected by wear and weather conditions, resulting in a shabby appearance that eventually prompted the RDAF to switch to a gloss finish which was more durable. *(Photo: RDAF)*

◄ Denmark operated a total of 51 Starfighters, the last examples being withdrawn in 1986. A batch of 15 F-104G and three TF-104G aircraft were transferred to Taiwan in 1987. *(Photo: RDAF)*

evaluation of many available types including the Phantom, Mirage, Lightning and others, but with the Starfighter already in AMI service, Lockheed's proposal for a derivative of the F-104 (Model CL-980) was always the most suitable option and on 26 January 1966, the AMI officially chose the definitive F-104S as their future fighter. The first F-104S was actually a modified Fiat-built F-104G (MM6658) used as an aerodynamic prototype (making its first flight on 22 December 1966) although a second prototype (MM6660 fitted with new avionics systems) first flew on 28 February 1967. The first production F-104S built by Aeritalia (MM6660) completed its maiden flight on 30 December 1968. Designed to carry AIM-7 Sparrow missiles (hence the 'S' designation) the internal Vulcan gun was deleted in the

dedicated interceptor version, primarily to save weight. With an additional weapons pylon for a Sparrow missile under each wing plus two further attachment points under the forward fuselage, the F-104S had nine hard points in all and could carry up to seven 227 kg (500lb) bombs – a weapons capability that was a great improvement over the F-104G, and sufficient to enable the F-104S to act as a fully versatile multi-role machine. Despite these improvements and some internal structural strengthening, the external appearance of the F-104S airframe was almost identical to the F-104G, differing only in the addition of a ventral strake under each side of the rear fuselage, and the replacement of the air intake auxiliary doors with new (larger) doors than hinged downwards. The new intake doors were

necessary for the increased demands of the J79-GE-19 engine that was adopted for this variant, delivering 13 percent more power (17,900lb). Although many sources suggest that the F-104 intake shape was changed, it was in fact unchanged, save for a slight reduction in the forward extent of the intake lip, which was reduced by just 23.4mm. Theoretically an F-104S could be equipped with four or five bombs, two tanks and two AIM-9s, thereby becoming what would now be referred-to as a "swing role" aircraft. Italy's aerospace industry was ultimately responsible for 65 percent of the programme cost, with Aeritalia manufacturing the airframes, Fiat producing the engines under a license agreement, and Selenia undertaking license production of the Sparrow IIM missile. Milan-based FIAR produced the NASARR R21-G radar (derived from the earlier F-15A system) under an agreement reached with NAA. The new F-104S variant entered service during 1969, and a fleet of 205 aircraft was delivered from 1969 onwards in either interceptor or fighter-bomber configuration. The last of Italy's single-seat F-104Gs were withdrawn from service in 1983, but the F-104S (and TF-104G trainers) remained in service until 1984 when the AMI finally withdrew the last of its Starfighters following deliveries of Eurofighter Typhoons. The F-104S-ASA (Aggiornamento Sistemi d'Arma or Weapon Systems Update) comprised 147 aircraft modified from existing airframes, upgraded with Fiat R21G/M1 radar with frequency hopping, look-down/shoot-down capability, new IFF and weapons delivery computer, and provision for AIM-9L all-aspect Sidewinder and Selenia Aspide missiles. Due to the delays of Aspide integration, it was also called the ASA-1 with Sparrows, and ASA-2 when the Aspide became available, and eventually all F-104Ss were upgraded to ASA-2 standard. The fighter-bombers had no substantial improvements, and were later modified to interceptor standard without the M61. The F-104S-ASA/M (Modified) consisted of 49 F-104S-ASA and 15 two-seat TF-104G aircraft that were upgraded from 1998 to ASA/M standard with GPS, new TACAN and Litton LN-30A2 INS, refurbished airframe, and improved cockpit displays. All strike-related equipment was removed. As the last Starfighters in combat service, they were withdrawn in October 2004 from service with 10° Gruppo/9° Stormo.

Italy

Aeronautica Militare Italiana
3° Stormo, Villafranca
28° Gruppo
132° Gruppo
4° Stormo, Grosseto
9° Gruppo
20° Gruppo
5° Stormo, Rimini
23° Gruppo
102° Gruppo
6° Stormo, Ghedi
154° Gruppo
36° Stormo, Gioia del Colle
12° Gruppo
156° Gruppo
37° Stormo, Grazzanise
10° Gruppo
51° Stormo, Treviso / Istrana
22° Gruppo
155° Gruppo
53° Stormo, Cameri
21° Gruppo

This elevated view of the F-104S illustrates the position of the additional outer wing pylons that were incorporated into this variant for the Sparrow missile. *(Photo: Alenia)*

Delivered in an unpainted condition with white wings, Italy's Starfighters were soon camouflaged, the distinctive fuselage code numbers changed to white. The first Italian F-104G completed its maiden flight on 9 June 1962 and it wasn't until 5 October 1962 that the first Fiat/Aeritalia– manufactured example made its initial flight. *(Photo: Tim McLelland collection)*

Italy received 105 F-104G aircraft, 24 TF-104G and 20 RF-104G aircraft, together with 205 F-104S aircraft (as illustrated) and a further batch of six former Luftwaffe TF-104Gs. By 1986 the Aeronautica Militare Italiana was the largest operator of the F-104. *(Photo: Tim McLelland)*

Norway

The Kongelige Norske Luftforsvaret (Royal Norwegian Air Force) received the first of sixteen Lockheed-built F-104Gs (as part of MAP arrangements) during 1963. These were followed by a further three Canadair-built F-104Gs, and two Lockheed-built TF-104Gs. The fleet of F-104Gs was converted to RF-104G reconnaissance standard, assigned to No.331 Skvadron based at Bodo, but when reconnaissance-configured RF-5As were delivered to No.717 Skvadron, the Starfighters reverted to the standard fighter configuration. Two former Luftwaffe TF-104Gs were later transferred to Norway from the Nato training

fleet based at Luke AFB in the USA. During 1973, a second KNL Starfighter unit (No.334 Skvadron) was formed with 18 former Royal Canadian Air Force CF-104s together with four CF-104D trainers. These aircraft were modified to carry Martin Bullpup air-to-surface missiles and employed in the anti-shipping role.

Operations continued until 1983 when the remaining active aircraft (the former RCAF machines) were withdrawn. Most aircraft were placed in storage although at least 12 aircraft were transferred to Turkey. Having amassed over 56,000 flying hours during their service, it was remarkable that only six aircraft were lost in flying accidents.

Royal Norwegian Air Force
331 Squadron based at Bodø
334 Squadron based at Bodø

Canada

Canada's requirement for an aircraft to replace the F-86 Sabre led to a competition for a new fighter-bomber, although Canada's primary requirement was for a nuclear strike and reconnaissance platform. The F-4 Phantom, Buccaneer, Mirage, F-105, Starfighter and F11F-1F Super Tiger were considered and the RCAF expressed its preference for either Phantom or F-105, but cost and timescale issued eventually persuaded the RCAF to turn its attention to the Super Tiger, even though it was in affect a "paper" design that had not even been purchased by the US Navy. However on 2 July 1959 it was announced that Canada had chosen the F-104 Starfighter, having secured a satisfactory arrangement for license production of the aircraft in Canada, plus the manufacture of almost complete airframes for Germany's Luftwaffe. On 14 August it was announced that Canadair of Montreal had been selected to manufacture 200 aircraft for the RCAF under license from Lockheed, together with the wings, tail assemblies, and rear fuselage sections for 66 Lockheed-built Starfighters that were destined for the Luftwaffe (a license production contract was signed on 17 September). Designated as the CF-111 by the RCAF and CL-90 by Canadair,

During 1974 the Royal Norwegian Air Force acquired a batch of 18 CF-104 and four CF-104D trainers from the Canadian Armed Forces. These aircraft retained their CAF camouflage colours, with Norwegian serials and insignia applied. *(Photo: Tim McLelland collection)*

the aircraft was eventually designated as the CF-104 by all parties. In effect, the CF-104 was a Canadian-built F-104G, fitted with equipment suitable for the RCAF's requirements and optimized for the nuclear strike role. With NASARR R-24A equipment dedicated to the air-to-ground mode, the main landing gear legs were fitted with longer-stroke liquid springs and carried larger tyres. The CF-104 also retained provision for the removable refuelling probe designed for the USAF's F-104C. Provision was made for a ventral reconnaissance pod equipped with four Vinten cameras, and although the aircraft was configured for conventional ground attack duties, the 20mm M61A1 cannon was removed, chiefly because the aircraft's primary role would be the delivery of a single US-supplied nuclear bomb. Orenda Engines secured a license agreement to build the J79-OEL-7 engine, rated at 15,800lb (with afterburner). Lockheed supplied F-104A-15-LO 56-0770 to Canada to act as a pattern aircraft for CF-104 manufacture and although it was fitted with CF-104 fire control systems and flight control equipment, the airframe was not strengthened to F-104G standard. The first Canadair-constructed CF-104 (RCAF 12701) was airlifted to Palmdale early in1961, where it made its first flight on 26 May. The second CF-104 (12702) also made its first flight at Palmdale, the first two CF-104s to fly from Canadair's Montreal facility being Nos.12703 and 12704, both taking to the air on 14 August 1961. The 200th and last CF-104 to be manufactured (12900) was completed in September 1963 before being delivered to the RCAF on 10 January 1964. Canadair then began production of Starfighters for Nato countries, under MAP arrangements. Eight RCAF CF-104 squadrons were assigned to Europe as part of No.1 Air Division and other

Norway's initial Starfighter fleet was established in 1963 when 19 F-104G aircraft were delivered from Canadair, together with four TF-104G trainers, under a Military Assistance Programme arrangement. The Starfighter remained in service with the Norwegian Air Force until late 1982.*(Photo: Mick Freer)*

Canada operated a relatively large fleet of 200 CF-104s (all built by Canadair) together with 38 CF-104D trainers manufactured by Lockheed. Initial service entry was in 1962. Aircraft were supplied with white-painted wing surfaces, onto which the Royal Canadian Air Force's flamboyant markings were applied. Aircraft assigned to trials and training acquired additional high-visibility red markings. *(Photo: Tim McLelland collection)*

Although a number of RCAF aircraft were assigned to reconnaissance, the RCAF didn't obtain any RF-104G aircraft. Standard CF-104 aircraft were fitted with a purpose-designed Vinten reconnaissance pod fixed under the fuselage, containing four cameras. *(Photo: Tim McLelland collection)*

Canadair CF-104
104838

No.439 Squadron
Canadian Armed Forces
CFB Baden–Soellingen
1977 Tiger Meet

FANGS OF DEATH

Illustration by Ted Williams

than an OCU based in Canada (eventually becoming No.417 Squadron), RCAF's aircraft were all committed to the nuclear deterrent role in Europe. By 1968 the force had been reduced to four nuclear strike squadrons and two tactical reconnaissance squadrons. The nuclear strike role was abandoned during 1970, and this prompted the modification of the CF-104 fleet to resume use of the 20mm Vulcan cannon and the use of both twin bomb ejector rack carriers and multi-tube rocket launchers. By 1983, all single-seat CF-104s had been modified with a Litton LW-33 digital inertial navigation and attack system, which replaced the aircraft's LN-3 analog inertial navigation system. After a long and successful service life, the last CF-104s were finally withdrawn in March 1986. Most aircraft were placed in storage pending disposal although some airframes were eventually transferred to Turkey for further use. Canada's accident rate was undoubtedly high, with 110 aircraft being lost from a fleet of 239 aircraft. However the RCAF (Canadian Armed Forces) aircraft generally accrued much higher hours than any other country, with many aircraft recording more than 6,000 hours – as compared to perhaps only 2,000 hours for a Luftwaffe machine. In this context, the CF-104 proved to be no less reliable than any of its counterparts.

Thre CF-104s from Nos. 421, 441 and 439 Squadrons, each wearing a special anniversary colour scheme during 1983. *(Photo: CAF)*

Royal Canadian Air Force
Canadian Armed Forces
1 Wing RCAF, Marville/Lahr
No. 439 (Sabre-Toothed Tiger) Squadron
No. 441 (Silver Fox) Squadron
2 Wing RCAF, Grostenquin/Baden-Söllingen/Lahr
No. 421 (Red Indian) Squadron
No. 430 (Silver Falcon) Squadron
3 Wing RCAF, Grostenquin/Baden-Söllingen/Zweibrücken
No. 427 (Lion) Squadron
No. 434 (Bluenose) Squadron
4 Wing RCAF, Baden-Söllingen
No. 422 (Tomahawk) Squadron
No. 444 (Cobra) Squadron
Central Experimental and Proving Establishment/Aerospace Engineering and Test Establishment
6 Strike-Recce OTU
No. 417 Operational Training Squadron RCAF

Greece
Greece's Elliniki Vassiliki Aeroporia (Royal Hellenic Air Force) was allocated 35 Canadair-built F-104Gs and four Lockheed-built TF-104Gs as part of the MAP re-equipment process, and deliveries began during 1964. A further ten MAP-funded (Lockheed-built) F-104Gs and two TF-104Gs were later delivered to Greece from existing USAF stocks. The Starfighters were assigned to 335 Mira "Tiger" Squadron as part of the 114th Pterix (Wing), based at Tanagra. Once that

Line up of CAF CF-104s at Baden-Sollingen under a typically grey European sky. Although the CAF suffered a high Starfighter loss rate, almost half of the crashes were directly attributable to poor weather conditions. Also visible in this photograph are the radar warning receiver modifications fitted (during the 1980s) under the CF-104's nose and tail. *(Photo: CAF)*

unit was fully established, No.336 "Olympus" Mira (part of the 116th Wing at Araxos) also re-equipped with Starfighters. These two squadrons were initially dedicated to the nuclear strike roles within the 1st Tactical Air Force as a part of Greece's commitment to NATO, but they were re-assigned to the conventional strike role during the early 1970s. A batch of nine F-104Gs was delivered from Spain in 1972, together with two TF-104Gs from Germany in 1977, all provided as attrition replacements. Further aircraft arrived in 1982 when ten Fiat-built F-104Gs were transferred from the Netherlands, and

these were followed by yet more aircraft from Germany, as former Luftwaffe and Marineflieger Starfighters were withdrawn from service and sent to Greece as part of Bonn's "Minerva" military aid program that was agreed with Greece. This eventually comprised 22 RF-104Gs, 38 F-104Gs, and 20 TF-104Gs, although some of these aircraft were held in storage or used as spares sources.

Hellenic Air Force
335 Moira "Tigris", Tanagra/Araxos
336 Moira "Olympos", Tanagra/Araxos

As part of a Military Assistance Programme, Greece received 45 F-104G aircraft together with six TF-104G aircraft (illustrated). Additional aircraft were eventually acquired from other Starfighter operators, with 79 being supplied by Germany, seven from the Netherlands and nine from Spain. *(Photo: Tim McLelland collection)*

Like their Italian, Belgian and Canadian counterparts, Greece participated in the Nato's annual Tiger Meets with their Starfighters. F-104G 63-2720 was suitably decorated with black and yellow tiger stripes. *(Photo: Hellenic Air Force)*

To mark the end of Greece's Starfighter operations F-104G 7151 was repainted in an eye-catching paint scheme. This contrasted with the dull colours that was applied to the rest of Greece's Starfighter fleet, all of which were painted in USAF-style camouflage. *(Photo: Hellenic Air Force)*

Turkey

The Turk Hava Kuvvetleri (THK) received an initial batch of 32 F-104Gs manufactured by Lockheed and Canadair in 1963, together with four TF-104Gs built by Lockheed. These aircraft equipped Nos.141 and 142 Filo, plus an Operational Conversion Unit based at Murted. During 1972 a batch of nine F-104Gs and two TF-104Gs was transferred to Turkey from Spain, and assigned to the 9th Wing at Murted. Two years later, a batch of 18 new-build F-104S interceptors arrived from Italy, having allegedly been funded by Libya in return for Turkish assistance in building up the Libyan Arab Republic Air Force. These aircraft were also delivered to the 9th Wing and during May of 1975 the order was increased to 40. It is believed that Turkish Starfighers participated in the 1976 Turkish invasion of Cyprus, but there is no evidence to suggest that Turkish and Greek Starfighters were ever engaged in direct conflict with each other. When the

Starfighter began its withdrawal from use within Europe, substantial numbers of aircraft were transferred from Belgium, Canada, Germany, Norway, Germany, and the Netherlands. The process began with 18 F-104Gs from Belgium in 1981, although these were withdrawn from use in 1987. Some 43 F-104Gs (including 22 RF-104Gs) and 10 TF-104Gs were transferred from the Netherlands and nine RF-104G, three CF-104s, and one TF-104G were transferred from Norway. A total of 170 former Luftwaffe Starfighters were transferred to Turkey and 52 CF-104s were transferred from Canada. Eventually, the Turkish Air Force acquired more than 400 Satrfighters although it is unclear how many were actually operated, as some aircraft were placed in storage and some were used as spares sources. Operated in both the air defence and ground attack role, the Starfighter was a major part of Turkey's offensive and defensive capability for many years, even though most of the

aircraft were gradually acquired almost by chance rather than design. The replacement process began in 1987 when the first F-16s were delivered to Turkey although it wasn't until 1996 that the final examples (former Canadian CF-104s) were withdrawn from use.

Türk Hava Kuvvetleri

4 Ana Jet Us, Akıncı
141 Filo
142 Filo
Öncel Filo
6 Ana Jet Us, Bandirma
161 Filo
162 Filo
8 Ana Jet Us, Diyarbakir
181 Filo
182 Filo
9 Ana Jet Us, Balikesir
191 Filo
192 Filo
193 Filo

Turkey's F-104Gs were supplied in unpainted condition (and did not feature the white-painted wings that were common to many other nations), although a variety of paint schemes were progressively applied to Turkey's Starfighter fleet, these often being carried-over from former operators from where the aircraft were obtained. *(Photo: Tim McLelland collection)*

Although Turkey received 48 new-build F-104Gs (and six TF-104Gs) in 1963, a large number of aircraft were also acquired from other Nato operators, including 170 examples from Germany and 52 from Canada. As illustrated here, the CF-104 aircraft were not repainted although some acquired tip tanks from Luftwaffe aircraft, complete with fluorescent orange tip markings. *(Photo: Tim McLelland collection)*

Spain

Lockheed manufactured 18 F-104Gs and three TF-104Gs for Spain, and these were supplied as part of MAP arrangements to Spain's Ejercito del Aire during 1965. Replacing F-86F Sabres of 61 Escuadron (part of Ala 6 at Torrejon), the single-seat examples were designated as the C.8 in Spanish service (serials C.8-1 to C.8-18) while the trainers were designated as the CE.8 (serials CE.8-1 to CE.8-3), although in practise the aircraft was referred-to as the F-104 Starfighter. The aircraft were operated successfully until 1972 when F-4 Phantonms were acquired, enabling the Starfighters to be returned to US control for eventual re-allocation. The Spanish Air Force earned the distinction of being the only Starfighter operator to boast a completely accident-free service record, with not a single aircraft being lost.

Ejército del Aire

Ala 6 based at Torrejon (later redesignated Ala 16
61 Escuadron (later redesignated 161 Escuadron and 104 Escuadron

Taiwan

The Republic of China Air Force (RoCAF) was a major operator of the Starfighter, using aircraft that were primarily acquired from other air forces. Ultimately, some 247 aircraft were acquired although not all were flown operationally. Many aircraft came from USAF stocks while others were transferred from the Luftwaffe and Danish Air Force, while others came from the Japanese Air Self Defense Force. The first aircraft arrived in May 1960 when the first of 24 former USAF F-104As and five F-104Bs were delivered. From 1964, further deliveries commenced and 46

Lockheed-manufactured F-104Gs were accompanied by eight TF-104Gs, together with a batch of 21 RF-104Gs manufactured by Canadair. A further six F-104Ds arrived in 1975 from the USA, these being former Air National Guard aircraft. Further deliveries took place in 1983 when 38 F-104Gs and 27 TF-104Gs were transferred from the Luftwaffe, although the aircraft came directly from the USA, having been used for training at Luke AFB. Four years later the RoCAF had received a batch of 22 F-104Js and five F-104DJs from Japan, together with a smaller batch of 15 F-104Gs and three TF-104Gs from Denmark. Some of these aircraft were assigned to Taiwan's operational Starfighter squadrons although most were probably used as spares sources. Details of Taiwan's Starfighter operations are scarce, although it is known that a pair of Starfighters were responsible for shooting

Turkey obtained six TF-104G trainers from Lockheed in 1963 although additional trainers were obtained from other Nato countries in the 1970s and 1980s. The original new-build aircraft were delivered unpainted. *(Photo: Tim McLelland collection)*

Spain's F-104s were supplied by the USA under a Military Assistance Programme arrangement. 18 F-104Gs were manufactured by Canadair and a further three TF-104Gs were built by Lockheed and all of these were delivered to the Ejerciti del Aire in 1965. *(Photo: Tim McLelland collection)*

down two MiG-19s during conflict with the People's Liberation Army, on 13 January 1967. Units equipped with the Starfighter were the 7th, 8th, and 28th Tactical Fighter Squadrons of the 427th TFW at CCK AB, the 41st, 42nd, 48th TFS of the 499th TFW at Hsinchu AB, and the 12th TRS at Taoyuan AB. Despite little

information on Taiwan's activities, the RoCAF was undoubtedly one of the Starfighter's most significant users and it wasn't until 1998 that the last examples (RF-104Gs) were retired, when a ceremony was held at Ching Chuang Kang Air Base on 22 May. The first withdrawals were the F-104s of the 427th

TFW, which started to convert onto new F-CK-1s in 1993. In May 1997 the 499th TFW at Hsinchu AB started to replace its Starfighters with Mirage 2000s for the interceptor role. Before the Starfighter's final retirement, the 12th TRS was the sole F-104 operator, and the unit was relocated from Taoyuan AB to Hsinchu AB. The last two operational ROCAF Starfighters were TF-104G 4186 and 4196, departing Hsinchu on 8 May for the retirement ceremony.

Republic of China Air Force
427th Tactical Fighter Wing, Ching Chuang Kang AB
7th Tactical Fighter Squadron
8th Tactical Fighter Squadron
28th Tactical Fighter Squadron
35th Tactical Fighter Squadron
499th Tactical Fighter Wing, Hsinchu AB
41st Tactical Fighter Squadron
42nd Tactical Fighter Squadron
48th Tactical Fighter Squadron
401st Tactical Combined Wing, Taoyuan AB
12th Tactical Reconnaissance Squadron

Japan
It was first announced that Japan would acquire the Starfighter as its standard air superiority fighter during November 1960. An

Spain's Ejercito del Aire Starfighters boasted a completely crash-free record and the entire fleet was transferred to Greece and Turkey in 1972 when Spain acquired F-4 Phantoms. Despite flying more than 17,000 hours, no accidents occurred, probably because the aircraft were used only in the high altitude interceptor role in good weather conditions. *(Photo: Tim McLelland collection)*

Replacement of the ROCAF Starfighter fleet began in 1993 but it wasn't until May 1998 that the last operational unit (the 12th TRS) retired its last pair of aircraft, these being TF-104Gs 4186 and 4196. *(Photo: Tim McLelland collection)*

The Republic of China Air Force operated a fleet of 247 Starfighters, most being acquired from other countries where the aircraft was replaced by more modern aircraft. Aircraft came from the USAF, Germany, Canada, Japan, Denmark and Belgium, and ranged from early F-104A s through to RF-104Gs. TF-104G trainers were also obtained from various sources, and it is believed that from the overall total of 247 aircraft, a small proportion were not flown and were used as spares sources. *(Photo: Tim McLelland collection)*

industrial cartel headed by Mitsubishi Heavy Industries was given the responsibility for the license manufacture of the Starfighter in Japan, initially assembling aircraft that had been manufactured by Lockheed, but eventually shifting to full-scale manufacture of the aircraft, using components produced in Japan. Designated as the F-104J (the "J" denoting Japan), the aircraft was in effect a license-built F-104G. However, it was ostensibly geared towards the air-to-air defensive role, because of Japan's existing post-war treaty agreements that prevented the country form acquiring aircraft with any offensive capability. The F-104J was equipped with a J79-IHI-11A engine, manufactured under license by Ishikawajima-Harima. It featured an

Autonetics NASARR F-15J-31 fire control system optimized for the air-to-air mode, and was armed with the standard 20-mm M61A1 cannon together with up to four AIM-9 Sidewinder air-to-air missiles, with the usual wing attachment points and provbision for a twin launcher under the forward fuselage. The first Lockheed-built F-104J (Model 683-07-14) flew for the first time on 30 June 1961. The first three F-104Js were built and assembled by Lockheed, after which a further 29 examples were shipped to Japan in disassembled form for assembly by Mitsubishi. Further Starfighter production was then assigned to Mitsubishi, with a total of 178 Mitsubishi-manufactured F-104Js being delivered from March of 1965 until 1967. The F-104DJ (Model 583B-10-17) was

the two-seat trainer version of the F-104J for Japan, featuring electronics and systems that were compatible with those of the single-seat version. Twenty examples of the F-104DJ were manufactured for assembly in Japan beginning in July 1962 and January 1964 (Lockheed manufactured every F-104DJ destined for Japan). Entering service with the Koku Jietai (Japanese Air Self Defense Force) in October 1966, the first JASDF units to convert to the F-104J were the 201st and 202nd Fighter Interceptor Squadrons (Hiko-tais) based at Chitose and Nyutabaru. Some 210 F-104Js and 20 F-104DJ operational trainers were delivered to the JASDF and all were used exclusively in the interceptor role. It is believed that 34 F-104Js and two F-104DJs were destroyed in flying

The Japanese Air Self Defense Force operated a fleet of 210 F-104J aircraft in the interceptor role, together with 20 F-104DJ twin-seat trainers. Deliveries began in 1962 and the aircraft remained in service until 1986 and only three aircraft were lost during this period (two were lost in a mid-air collision). This remarkabvle safety record contrasts with the Starfighter's poor reputation, caused primarily by the low-level environment in which many Starfighters operated, often in terrible weather conditions. *(Photo: JASDF)*

The JASDF Starfighters were distributed between seven fighter squadrons and although the aircraft were never used in combat, many interceptions of intruding Soviet aircraft were performed. The last aircraft to remain in JASDF service were F-104J aircraft converted to unmanned target drone configuration. *(Photo: JASDF)*

accidents, but the JASDF was undoubtedly sarisfied with the performance and reliability of the Starfighter, and it wasn't until March 1986 that the last aircraft was withdrawn. Most aircraft were placed in storage pending disposal although at least 27 aircraft were transferred to Taiwan for further use.

Japan Air Self-Defense Force
2nd Kokudan, Chitose Air Base (201st) and Komatsu Air Base (203rd)
201st Hikōtai
203rd Hikōtai
5th Kokudan, Nyutabaru Air Base (202nd) and Tsuiki Air Base (204th)
202nd Hikōtai
204th Hikōtai
6th Kokudan, Komatsu Air Base

205th Hikōtai
7th Kokudan, Hyakuri Air Base, part at Naha Air Base
206th Hikōtai
207th Hikōtai

Germany
(see main chapter 5)
Luftwaffe
Aufklärungsgeschwader 51 "Immelmann" Ingolstadt/Manching
Aufklärungsgeschwader 52, Leck
Jagdbombergeschwader 31 "Boelcke", Nörvenich
Jagdbombergeschwader 32, Lechfeld
Jagdbombergeschwader 33, Büchel
Jagdbombergeschwader 34, Memmingen
Jagdbombergeschwader 36, Rheine-Hopsten

Jagdgeschwader 71 "Richthofen", Wittmundhaven
Jagdgeschwader 74, Neuburg
Marineflieger
Marinefliegergeschwader 1, Schleswig-Jagel
Marinefliegergeschwader 2, Eggebeck

Jordan
(see main chapter 5)
Royal Jordanian Air Force
No. 9 Squadron, Prince Hassan Air Base
No. 25 Squadron, Mwaffaq Salti

Pakistan
(see main chapter 5)
Pakistan Air Force
No. 9 Air Superiority Squadron based at Sargodha

This interesting in-flight photograph illustrates the two camouflage paint schemes that were applied to Luftwaffe aircraft. The first (in the background) was introduced during the a960s and this remained in use until the 1980s when a new camouflage pattern was introduced, as seen in the foreground. *(Photo: Tim McLelland collection)*

Unlike their Luftwaffe counterparts, the German Navy maintained just one standard paint scheme for its aircraft, as illustrated. The markings of Marinefliegergeschwader 2 are clearly visible on the aircraft's tail, together with the distinctive "Marine" titles that were applied to the rear fuselage. Despite being designed as a high-altitude fighter, the F-104G performed remarkably well in the low-level anti-shipping role. *(Photo: Alf Blume)*

F-104G 683D-8100 was manufactured by Fokker during 1963. It was delivered to the Luftwaffe in 1964 but subsequently withdrawn from use and leased to MBB for a Control Configured Vehicle (CCV) and fly-by-wire technologies research programme. The aircraft's natural stability was replaced with computer controlled fly-by wire system that allowed the aircraft to be flown in unstable condition, and a second tail unit was attached in canard configuration as part of this process. The test program ended in April 1984 and this unique aircraft was transferred to the Wehrtechnisches Museum at Koblenz. *(Photo: MBB)*

The National Aeronautics & Space Administration (Nasa) operated a total of 11 Starfighters between 1956 and 1994. Used for scientific research and in support of other aircraft programmes, they were also used for astronaut training as part of the USAF's NF-104 project and in direct support of Nasa's space programme. The Space Shutte's thermal tiles were tested on the F-104 and many other well-known projects relied on support from the Starfighter fleet, including the X-15 and the Lifting Body project. The aircraft were originally delivered unpainted, but Nasa soon applied distinctive yellow and fluorescent orange markings on most aircraft. This colour scheme eventually gave way to the standard Nasa white finish, complete with Nasa's famous badge placed on the aircraft's air intakes. *(Photos: Nasa)*

USA

(see main chapter 2)
United States Air Force
Air Force Systems Command
U.S. Air Force Aerospace Research Pilot School (ARPS), Edwards AFB
Tactical Air Command
479th Tactical Fighter Wing, George AFB
434th Tactical Fighter Squadron
435th Tactical Fighter Squadron
436th Tactical Fighter Squadron
476th Tactical Fighter Squadron
Air Defense Command/Aerospace Defense Command
56th Fighter-Interceptor Squadron,

Wright-Patterson AFB
83d Fighter Interceptor Squadron, Hamilton AFB
337th Fighter Interceptor Squadron, Westover AFB
538th Fighter-Interceptor Squadron, Larson AFB
319th Fighter-Interceptor Squadron, Homestead AFB
331st Fighter-Interceptor Squadron, Webb AFB
482d Fighter-Interceptor Squadron, Homestead AFB
Air National Guard
161st Fighter Interceptor Group, Arizona Air

National Guard based, Sky Harbor ANGB/Sky Harbor International Airport
197th Fighter Interceptor Squadron
156th Fighter Group, Puerto Rico Air National Guard, Muniz ANGB/San Juan International Airport, Puerto Rico
198th Tactical Fighter Squadron
169th Fighter Interceptor Group, South Carolina Air National Guard, McEntire ANGB
157th Fighter Interceptor Squadron
134th Fighter Interceptor Group, Tennessee Air National Guard, McGhee Tyson ANGB
151st Fighter Interceptor Squadron

F-104A 56-0790 was delivered to the USAF in 1957 but it was soon transferred on loan to Nasa's Dryden Flight Research Center. It was then returned to Lockheed where it was fitted with a larger tail (as designed for the TF-104G) and used for atomic weapons shape trails. It was then used as a chase plane in support of the SR-71 Blackbird programme. Most unusually, it was subsequently fitted with new radar as part of developmental work for the F-104S programme, and this necessitated a replacement radome, taken from the Lockheed U-2 (as illustrated). The radome fitted perfect as the U-2 was developed directly from the F-104. *(Photo: Lockheed)*

▶ The Lockheed CL-1200 Lancer was a company-funded proposal for a new and improved Lockheed F-104 Starfighter. It was intended for the export market direct competition with the F-5E, Mirage F1, YF-17 and the F-4. It featured a new high-mounted, increased span wing and low-mounted, enlarged tailplanes. Both features were incorporated to improve flight handling characteristics and short-field performance. The CL1200-1 was to have used an uprated version of the General Electric J79 with a later variant known as the CL1200-2 to be powered by a Pratt and Whitney TF-30 turbofan. The CL-1200-1 was entered in the International Fighter Aircraft competition, but when the Northrop F-5 was chosen as the winner in November 1970, the primary market for the Lancer was lost, and the project was terminated. *(Photo: Lockheed)*

Lockheed F-104 Starfighter variants

XF-104
Two prototypes with Wright J65 engines. One aircraft equipped with M61 cannon as an armament test bed. Both aircraft destroyed in crashes.

YF-104A
17 pre-production aircraft used for engine, equipment, and flight testing.

F-104A
153 initial production versions. In 1967 some F-104As and Bs re-fitted with J79-GE-19 engines rated at 17,900lb.

NF-104A
Three aircraft with an additional 6,000 lb Rocketdyne LR121/AR-2-NA-1 rocket engine, used for astronaut training.

QF-104A
22 F-104As converted into radio-controlled unmanned drones.

F-104B
Tandem two-seat, dual-control trainer version of F-104A. 26-built.

F-104C
Fighter-bomber variant for USAF Tactical Air Command, with improved fire-control radar. Designed to carry one Mk 28 or Mk 43 nuclear weapon on a centerline pylon. F-104C also had in-flight refuelling capability.

F-104D
Dual-control trainer version of F-104C. 21 built.

F-104DJ
Dual-control trainer version of F-104J for Japanese Air Self-Defense Force. 20 built by Lockheed and assembled by Mitsubishi.

F-104F
Dual-control trainer based on F-104D, using the upgraded engine of the F-104G. No radar fitted. Produced as interim trainers for the German Air Force. 30 manufactured.

F-104G
1,122 aircraft produced as multi-role fighter-bombers. Manufactured by Lockheed, and under license. Featured strengthened fuselage and wing structure, increased internal fuel capacity, an enlarged vertical fin, strengthened landing gear with larger tyres, and revised flaps. Upgraded avionics included new radar and an infrared sight.

RF-104G
Tactical reconnaissance models based on F-104G. 189 examples manufactured.

TF-104G
Combat-capable trainer version of F-104G. 220 aircraft built. No cannon armament or centerline pylon, and reduced internal fuel capacity.

F-104H
Projected export version based on F-104G with simplified equipment and optical gun sight.

F-104J
Interceptor version of the F-104G for the JASDF, built under license by Mitsubishi. Some converted to UF-104J target drone standard. 210 built.

F-104N
Three F-104Gs delivered to NASA in 1963 for use as high-speed chase aircraft.

F-104S
Improved version of F-104G with a modified engine and Sparrow missile capability. 246 examples built. Two additional wing and two fuselage weapons points, more powerful J79-GE-19 engine with 17,900 lb thrust, and two additional ventral fins to increase stability. M61 cannon sacrificed to make room for missile avionics. Gun retained for fighter-bomber variants.

F-104S-ASA
Upgrade programme for 150 F-104S with Fiat R21G/M1 radar. Provision for AIM-9L and Selenia Aspide missiles.

F-104S-ASA/M
49 airframes upgraded in 1998 to ASA/M standard with GPS, new TACAN and Litton LN-30A2 INS, refurbished airframe, improved cockpit displays.

CF-104
Canadian-manufactured version of F-104G, built under license by Canadair. Cannon deleted (restored after 1972), additional internal fuel cell, and Canadian J79-OEL-7 engines with 15,800 lb thrust.

CF-104D
38 dual-control trainer versions of CF-104, built by Lockheed, but with Canadian J79-OEL-7 engines.

General characteristics (F-104G)
Crew: 1
Length: 54 ft 8 in (16.66 m)
Wingspan: 21 ft 9 in (6.36 m)
Height: 13 ft 6 in (4.09 m)
Wing area: 196.1 sq ft (18.22 m²)
Airfoil: Biconvex 3.36% root and tip
Empty weight: 14,000 lb (6,350 kg)
Loaded weight: 20,640 lb (9,365 kg)
Max. takeoff weight: 29,027 lb (13,170 kg)
Powerplant: 1 × General Electric J79-GE-11A afterburning turbojet
Dry thrust: 10,000 lbf (48 kN)
Thrust with afterburner: 15,600 lbf (69 kN)
Zero-lift drag coefficient: 0.0172
Drag area: 3.37 sq ft (0.31 m²)
Aspect ratio: 2.45

Performance
Maximum speed: 1,328 mph (Mach 2.01, 1,154 kn, 2,137 km/h)
Combat radius: 420 mi (365 nmi, 670 km)
Ferry range: 1,630 mi (1,420 nm, 2,623 km)
Service ceiling: 50,000 ft (15,000 m)
Rate of climb: 48,000 ft/min (244 m/s)
Wing loading: 105 lb/(sq ft) (514 kg/m²)
Thrust/weight: 0.54 with max. take off weight (0.76 loaded)
Lift-to-drag ratio: 9.2